THE COURTIERS OF
HENRY VIII

By the same author

Henry VIII

THE COURTIERS OF
HENRY VIII

DAVID MATHEW

EYRE & SPOTTISWOODE · LONDON

First published 1970
© *1970 David Mathew*
Printed in Great Britain for
Eyre & Spottiswoode (Publishers) Ltd
11 New Fetter Lane, EC4
by The Bowering Press, Plymouth

SBN 413 27300 8

15 July 11

16 2

Father & Son

FOR
GERVASE MATHEW

fratri unico, amico optimo

Contents

Appendices

Illustrations

Preface

This book attempts to give a fresh or at any rate an individual approach to a subject, which has been often before considered, the reign of Henry VIII. This is seen through an examination of the lives of his courtiers and includes a consideration of his greater ministers and especially of Thomas Cromwell upon whose period of rule so much of this reign hinges. In this matter it is important to escape from the effect of those denominational sympathies which dominated English writers of both Communions until at any rate the death of Pollard.

It is one of the consequences of the indifference towards the disputing parties which is found in the second half of the present century that we can now discern, as our forefathers could not, how many men of that period had an interior lack of interest in such disputes.

I suppose that what one really needs in an approach to any series of historical events is the possession of imaginative sympathy. In this case one feels especially I think for those whose high position had left them friendless like Thomas Cromwell and Anne Boleyn. Both came in time to have one solitary supporter, the sovereign who destroyed them. There comes over very clearly both John Fisher's fidelity and Thomas Cranmer's quiet hesitancy and lack of courage. Neither was made for enduring worldly success in the sixteenth century.

What made for success in those years was hardly virtue. It was rather a mixture of toughness and sober calculation like the character of the third Duke of Norfolk whose prudence, self-confidence and a certain tortuous secrecy had hoisted his family to the leadership of the Tudor aristocracy. This was in contrast to the Duke of Buckingham, who had failed like some mastodon from the dead centuries and who also possessed that curious concentration on hereditary grandeur so difficult for us now to understand. That was a quality which also marked his grandson, the poet Surrey.

As a group the courtiers were marked by a clear-sighted determination to increase their fortune and the greatest benefit that
came their way was the many thousand acres of monastic property.
This was the matter nearest to their thoughts and interests. Land
had a reality quite different from the King's own deliberations on
doctrinal questions. There was in all their lives a certain solitari-
ness. This great increase in worldly possessions was something that
came upon them unexpectedly. It descended suddenly like a
golden rain. It was greed of course that made them solitary.

Where evidence is comparatively slender we are fortunate to
possess the magnificent drawings of so many of the Henrican
courtiers from Holbein's pencil. They carry a very real conviction
of untrammelled fidelity. It was lucky that his first subjects had
belonged to the mercantile patriciate of Basel. He always very
clearly understood the influence of the growth of money-power.

In contrast to the world of these modern courtiers there went the
developing tragedy of the representatives of the old royal family,
what can for convenience be called the White Rose lines. The two
Queens of the South, Catherine of Aragon and at a later day
Catherine of Braganza, both failed to understand the character of
the northern nation. The Princess of Aragon however understood
these ancient stocks.

The position of this group of families has required the setting
down of a good deal of genealogical detail in order to make plain
the exact position. It is also difficult to get the White Rose families
into focus. So much of the earlier portions of their reign suffers
from the lack of surviving personal correspondence. There is an
absence of the sidelights that we are used to in the succeeding
centuries. There are also relatively few existing buildings.

King Henry's reign was passed in the Home Counties and it is
here that there can still be found the faint reflections of the background of his courtiers' lives; the Tudor brickwork on the outside
of the interior parts that the Cardinal erected at Hampton Court,
the great tower which still rises from the level land at Layer
Marney southwards from Colchester, and most of all the long gallery on the first floor of the Vyne, the house which the courtier
Lord Sandys built by the head waters of the Loddon quite close to
Basingstoke. Here on the linen-fold panelling there are worked out

the bearings of Sandys and of his sovereign. On one panel there is inscribed in honour of Queen Catherine a pomegranate issuing from a rose and up above, the castles of Castile. In his glorious youth the King came hunting here.

Away in the West on the water meadows beside the Severn, there lie the walls and stranded towers of Thornbury, all that remains of the families of the White Rose.

And here I must describe the meaning that I attach to the word 'Courtiers' in the title of this study. The Court was composed of men of a certain standing whose posts brought them into contact with the sovereign. Some great families like the Howards and the Greys, which is why these two are examined in some detail, were associated with the Court throughout the reign. The immediate courtiers included certain great officers of State, like the Earl Marshal, and then all those who served the King in the royal palaces through all the grades down to the youngest pages. The soldiers, as opposed to the officers, of the guard, the keepers of the wardrobe, the cooks and staffs of the royal kitchens can be regarded as the servants of the Court. They do not come within the subject of this volume.

All the new peers had some contact with the Court and this was also true of the great body of the peerage. There were, however, certain lords, particularly the less wealthy elements of those in the North Country, whose contacts with the Court were very faint and also intermittent. The officers of the State, all appointed by the King, must be counted among the courtiers during the years in which they held office beneath the Crown.

There were a few men whose situation was exceptional. Many of the bishops were throughout their lives the King's true servants. John Fisher, Bishop of Rochester was in an unusual position. He had been intimately associated with the ideas and also with the management of the property of the Countess of Richmond, Henry VII's mother; but the austerity of his life kept him remote from his sovereign. He may almost be regarded in a way as a counter-courtier. Sir Thomas More, likewise, had a detachment not so much from the King as from the King's associates, which must also have placed him outside the real circle of the Court. For the normal courtier was a man who came to Court to make his fortune, who gave good service and such companionship as the King would accept. The King was the sun and in the Tudor Court his courtiers would of necessity revolve around him. Perhaps the most successful example of the true type of Henrican courtier was Charles Brandon. He joined the Court as one of the royal pages; he gained the King's firm friendship; he became the Duke of Suffolk and he ended his life shortly before his royal master.

It was a military Court and it was assumed that the King's courtiers were always ready to defend his honour on land or sea. It was also, although the King would not have recognized this fact, a trifle philistine. The courtiers, as a body, were of course in no sense responsible for the royal policy, but they were very quick to grasp the opportunities that offered for accumulation. An intense preoccupation with mundane profit did not easily consort with intellectual or indeed artistic interests. A concern for money values was something which was common form to all the courtiers.

The court changed very much through the years. There was an almost Castilian quality about the early period reinforced by certain English characteristics, the King's robust piety and his devotion to an outdoor life. His natural skill as a horseman and in sport was accompanied very pleasantly by a high good humour provided that his companions all tried their hardest and could not surpass him. These years seem like the close of a long summer, the ending of the Middle Ages in the South of England.

As the decades passed the King was wearied by those, who like the Howards, had been always at his elbow. He preferred the men whom he had nurtured and created in the sense of the papal phrase *ab eo creato* used of the range of cardinals who were the 'creatures' of a special reign. It was this that made his final years so autocratic and so powerful.

The courtiers, as opposed to the King's individual ministers, merely reflected the wishes of their royal master. The Field of the Cloth of Gold provides us with an opportunity to study the demands which the King's love of ceremonial made upon the more privileged of his subjects, while an examination of the Pilgrimage of Grace shows those military duties which were always expected from the men of the King's *entourage*.

A consideration of this period inevitably shows the nature and effects of the religious changes. One is left with the impression that these were of secondary consequence compared to the sharp pull of worldly interest. With this there comes an investigation of the ecclesiastics about the Court. It is interesting to study where that group of young priests who were to be taken into the royal service hived off from their companions. This subject enables us to reach down to the taproots in the country. There can be no accurate study of the courtiers, which deals solely with those who made that grade.

One matter dealt with lies admittedly outside the general thesis, the chapter on the merchants of the Steelyard. These men were foreigners resident in London and the King was always conscious of them. They were not, however, within the ambit of the Court. But no study of Holbein's work in England would be complete if they were omitted from consideration.

I must here express my gratitude to all those who have helped me to gain some understanding of the architectural background of King Henry's reign. And first of all I am grateful to Sherman Lord Camoys and to his wife for the years that I have spent at Stonor Park, the home of the Stonors, which had already been in their possession for many generations when Henry VIII began his reign. It was hidden deep in the woods at the southern end of the Chilterns and was then the headquarters of the Henrican courtier Sir Adrian Fortescue.

I wish to give my thanks to Joan Russell for taking me to the Delawarr Chantry in Boxgrove Church, to Joan Berkeley for taking me to Montacute, to Thomas and Beth Stonor for showing me Layer Marney and to Georgina Stonor for showing me the Vyne. I am grateful to Carrie Constable-Maxwell for taking me to Romsey, to Margaret Mathew who took me to Bradgate House and to Leslie Hope who went with me to Thornbury.

I also wish to remember those who helped at an earlier stage, Donna Nennella Carr who took me to the tombs and castle at Framlingham and Marie Kerr who took me to the ruined manor house at Wingfield. I went with W. A. Pantin to Compton Win-yates and with Hugh Arbuthnott to Berkeley Castle and with Elizabeth Longford to Penshurst. The late Francis Mathew took

me to Sutton Place and on a journey in the North of England the
late Bishop of Lancaster showed me Hornby.

I wish to express my gratitude to Tessa, Una and Carmen Dillon
for their constant and technical help in many aspects of the book's
production. I should also explain that I have in certain sections re-
printed small portions of earlier works, phrases from *Catholicism in
England*, my short essay on Bishop Fisher, passages from an article
on Thomas Cromwell, and some sentences from *The Reformation
and the Contemplative Life* which I wrote with my brother Gervase.
Lastly, like all my books, this new volume owes more than I can
say to my brother's guidance.

DAVID MATHEW

Stonor Park
1970

PART ONE

THE REIGN'S BEGINNING

I

The Opening Phases

The old King Henry VII, his weak frame quite worn out, had died on 21 April 1509 at the end of spring in his new palace up the river at Richmond, renamed in honour of his northern earldom. He had hoarded coin, something that his son the Prince of Wales would never do. It was obvious at once that the new sovereign was at war with all the architectural insufficiency that he had inherited.

The coronation and the marriage of Henry VIII with the Princess of Aragon took place in London in the early summer. The ceremonies foreshadowed one aspect of the reign; the streets hung with tapestries from Flanders; the conduits running wine; the great processions. The pageantry, derived in part from the Burgundian Court, was played out against the crude London buildings that survived from the fifteenth century. The young sovereign was in reaction against the tradition of the 'wise kings' of the immediate past, his own father Henry VII and Ferdinand of Aragon, and the exemplar of both, Louis XI with his universal and unassuaged suspicion; his economy and meanness; his *outré* superstition-ridden religious life. That King was, at least on the surface, everything against which Henry VIII reacted; his wretched accommodation at Plessis-les-Tours; his association only with Bourgeois and with the lower orders; his mean clothing and the little silver-image of Our Lady of Rocamadour that he kept in the front of his worn head-gear. Nevertheless Louis XI and Henry VIII had this in common; they were both princes who knew in their hearts that their power was absolute.

Henry VIII was a splendid horseman and very generous; he revelled in the popularity that his generosity aroused. He was for several generations the first King of England to build up a public image. He had that easy good will which buoyant health had brought to him. And at the beginning he was always kind towards his cousins, the old stocks who had the blood of the 'White Rose of the House of York'. The chief of these families were the Countess of Salisbury and her sons the Poles, the Courtenay Marquess of Exeter and the Stafford Duke of Buckingham, who had his own separate royal descent. The De La Pole Duke of Suffolk was already a prisoner in the Tower.

It has always seemed to me that it was the King's hesitation about his own descent that made him turn against them. His father's claim was through the legitimated stock of the House of Beaufort one of whom was King Henry VII's mother. It is, perhaps, wise to set down now what happened to the heads of these great families. Suffolk was executed in 1513 and Buckingham in 1521 and Exeter in 1538 and Lady Salisbury in 1541; in each case the possessions of the stock were confiscated. This is a background to the life at Court. In the King's character cheerfulness and suspicion were intertwined; he was perhaps not very imaginative, but certainly blood-thirsty. If this sounds severe, his reign need only be compared with that of his contemporary sovereigns Francis I and Charles V.

In general they were all old-fashioned families, the leaders sometimes strong in character, but mentally in most cases very sluggish. Their high descent had an appeal for Queen Catherine with her memories of the great Castilian houses; but they had little in common with the established high English families[1] or with all the rising men from the country gentry, who accepted the dynamism of King Henry's Court.

On 29 June, five days after the coronation, the King's grandmother Margaret Countess of Richmond and Derby died in the Abbot's House at Westminster. She was the last survivor of the Beaufort family; a little wizened woman of deep piety, who became the widow of her first husband at fifteen. She gave an

---

[1] There are few generalizations to which there are no exceptions and for instance in this case Thomas Manners, Lord Roos was the son of Anne St Leger the daughter and heiress of Anne Duchess of Exeter sister to Edward IV. He was later made a Knight of the Garter and given the earldom of Rutland, which had formerly been held by the Royal Family; but he had no connection in his actions with the 'White Rose' stocks.

example of that early child-bearing which had ruined the physique of the great houses.

In this last period of pre-Reformation England it seems that the life in the rich easy-going convents, such as Amesbury, had lost its appeal for the widowed queens and princesses. This was partly the result of the growing influence of the stricter Orders all gathered round the capital, the Carthusians, the Observantine Franciscans and the Bridgettines of Syon. The great ladies had connections with these groups, as Sir Thomas More himself had, from the outside.

There was one aspect in which the religious life in England was different from that on the Continent. There were here no wealthy convents requiring heraldic quarterings from choir novices such as those found in the German lands, nor had the great French religious houses, whose headships were confined to princesses of the blood royal, any counterparts in English life.

As a result hardly any of the daughters of the rich English families joined the Religious. They were all swept into the child marriages which were arranged for them.[1]

It is curious that in the network of marriages among the leading families in the period of the War of the Roses I have come across no record of suits of nullity. The third marriage of Margaret Beaufort was perhaps an extra example of the practical alliance. She gave her position as the mother of a claimant to the throne to her husband the elderly Lord Stanley, who became the first Earl of Derby. This brought him and his supporters to the side of her son Henry Tudor, Earl of Richmond at Bosworth Field. After her son's accession as Henry VII, the purpose of the marriage now accomplished, she separated from Lord Derby to give herself up to a life of prayer.

Her life was passed in the royal manor of Woking, where buildings had been erected by Edward IV. Henry VIII was later to add a gallery; but everything has now disappeared. Margaret is best remembered as the founder of the Lady Margaret chairs of divinity, and of Christ's and St John's colleges at Cambridge. She

[1] Only two of the House of York became nuns, Bridget the youngest daughter of Edward IV, who joined the community of Dartford, and her cousin Anne de la Pole, who became a Bridgettine at Syon. In both cases at the time of their entry into Religion their fathers were dead and there was no marriage in prospect.

spent her benefactions on these great works; but they may have been suggested to her by John Fisher, who became her confessor and was appointed on her recommendation to the see of Rochester. They belong to her later life and there are no traces of such gifts when her son first reached the throne.

Her example was not followed in any way by her grandson, but it was reflected in the intellectual life of his reign, in the later years of the Bishop of Rochester and in the household of Sir Thomas More and in the visits of Erasmus.

Lady Margaret was among the early patrons of printed books and she translated from the French a part of the *Imitatio Christi*. She lived to be sixty-six, at that period a considerable age. Her great inheritance, which she used wholly for her charities, came from an amalgamation of the Beaufort lands. She also built the fine tomb of her parents in Wimborne Minster and established there in their memory a chantry and free school.

Another example from the same religion-encrusted world could be observed in the Duchess of York's household at Berkhampstead Castle. It is interesting that, although this household belonged to the centre of the Yorkist allegiance in the long wars, there was still a close association with the Lady Margaret. The identity of the old privileged class was not broken by this internecine struggle.

Cicely, Duchess of York was the mother of Edward IV. She lived until 1495 and was thus in her last years the grandmother of the reigning Queen. Both households had the same concentration on Mass attendance.[1] The Lady Margaret[2] rose at five o'clock and heard four or five Masses before breakfast, while the Duchess got up at seven, and matins of the day were followed by matins from the Little Office of Our Lady. During the morning she assisted at three Low Masses. At Berkhampstead Castle the day ended with evensong chanted by the choir. At dinner, the midday meal, there was spiritual reading for the assembled company.[3]

On the one hand both these examples show how the chaplains

---

[1] Cf. the valuable study on 'The Piety of Cicely, Duchess of York' by C. A. J. Armstrong in *For Hilaire Belloc* (1942), pp. 73–94.

[2] 'Sermon on the month's mind for the Countess of Richmond', *English Works of John Fisher*, ed. J. E. B. Mayor, p. 294.

[3] For an example these included Hilton's *Contemplative and Active Life*, St Bonaventure's *Life of Christ* and *The Golden Legend*, C. A. J. Armstrong, op. cit., p. 79.

attached to the great households might be employed and they also indicate how the daily Mass at King Henry's Court would fall into its place. In the Catholic world this Court Catholicism would continue for the next two centuries; its final phase perhaps is seen in the attendance, as Saint-Simon tells us, of the courtiers at all the Masses celebrated in Louis XIV's presence at Versailles.

We can see how closely the 'White Rose' families were attached to the observance of the Old Religion. It may be that a natural conservatism had drawn together the old cumbrous monasticism and the ancient baronies. It was in these cases the survival of a relationship which had been long-established. The families of the squirearchy, at least those in touch with the Court, and the new Tudor peerage were very different. They in general were swift and acquisitive. It was not so much fidelity to ancient custom as a certain slowness of the mind which dominated the great families whose power had come down from the fifteenth century.

There is an example of the close ties which the great families had with the religious life in the Courtenay family in the Household Book of Catherine Countess of Devon,[1] who was the child of Edward IV and therefore a granddaughter of the Duchess of York. This volume dealt with the arrangements at the dower house of Columb John, which she maintained for her grandson the Marquess of Exeter. It records the glaziers coming from Exeter with coloured glass for the new chamber and the wagon-loads of Lenten fish. There was a whole series of monastic presents and, in consequence, of religious expenses; partridges and cherries, a cock-pheasant for St Thomas' Day, swans from the Abbot of Ford and venison from the monastery at Buckland. These two religious houses were far apart; but these were presents of consideration.

The steward would be sent in to the county town to buy May strawberries and to satisfy the superior of the Blackfriars. Offerings to the chief monasteries were made on feasts and there was a Requiem in June, the accustomed Masses on All Souls Day and a heavy stipend paid to the prior of the Dominicans in London 'for a year's singing for Lord William'. Certain other elements were more unusual. Friars preached before the Countess at her expense in the

---

[1] *Letters and Papers, Foreign and Domestic, of the reign of Henry VIII*, ed. Brewer, Gairdner and Brodie (1862–1910, 1920), vol. iv, part i, 1524–6.

elaborately furnished chapels which were attached to all the Courtenay houses. Rooms were reserved by the family in the nearest Blackfriars for their use in Lent and Advent. In the 'White Rose' families it was not only the women who kept up this strict observance. There was a parallel in Lady Salisbury's accommodations. In this small group the life of the fifteenth century went forward quite unchanged. Further, between the religious houses and these royal stocks there was a client-patron relationship which belonged in effect rather to conservatism than to religion. There was no parallel to such contacts with the monastic world as belonged to the new rich landed families.

What was the exact position of the 'White Rose' grouping? To begin with Henry VIII, and also, in particular, Queen Catherine were friendly to them. His attitude towards them veered in time. Suspicion was not something that belonged to his carefree youth; it came upon him as he practised kingship. His appetite for appreciation grew and his cousins had not that gift of swift whole-hearted praise that the 'new men' knew well how to offer to him. What the King would value above all was ready service, that careful preparedness to build up in every way the royal position. What he did not want was men and women already of high standing who stood with a certain stodginess around the throne. Like all in his great state he did not really need friends, he wanted service. This seems the heart of his difficulty.

The Lancastrian cause was in eclipse. The old royal line had been extinguished with the death of Henry VI in 1471. He left no immediate heirs; his only son was dead and he himself had been an only child. His two aunts, the Electress Palatine and the Queen of Denmark, had died childless as had their younger brothers. He was the last descendant of Henry IV, who had usurped the throne.

The claims of Henry Tudor second Earl of Richmond, who had been attained by Richard III in 1483 at the time of the Duke of Buckingham's conspiracy, were slender enough. In the summer of 1485 he was at Harfleur assembling a force. The only men of rank with him were the Marquess of Dorset and the Earl of Oxford, the latter's fortune was quite negligible.

The Earl's claim depended on his mother the Countess of Richmond, who had now married Lord Stanley as her third husband. She was the heir general of the House of Beaufort and claimed to be the heiress of John of Gaunt, Duke of Lancaster who was the third son of Edward III. The old royal line had come from this prince. Nevertheless there was a flaw in her position. Her grandfather, John Earl of Somerset, was the eldest son of the Beaufort family, the children of John of Gaunt by his mistress Catherine Swynford. At a later date the parents were married and the Beauforts were legitimated.

There were other circumstances to build up this claim but not to give it any further substance. Henry's grandfather Owen Tudor had married Catherine of France, the widowed Queen of Henry V. In consequence the first Earl of Richmond, who was granted that almost royal title which had been held as an appanage by the Duke of Brittany, had been the half-brother of Henry VI. In 1485 the young earl of Richmond had been an exile in Brittany and France for fourteen years. There was moreover a mass of nobles of the Lancastrian tradition who, with good fortune, he could call upon. In the male line he was of an old Welsh stock and he decided that in his attempt upon the throne, he would land in Wales where he knew that Sir Rhys ap Thomas would rally to him.

Richmond was at this time twenty-eight and still unmarried. If he was to succeed not only in dethroning Richard III, but also in bringing to an end the long see-saw of these civil wars it was essential that he should marry the senior co-heiress of the rival house. On the previous Christmas Day in Rennes Cathedral he had solemnly promised to marry Elizabeth the eldest daughter of Edward IV, who was then nineteen.

We must now return from the House of Tudor to the House of York. The War of the Roses had broken out in 1454; it was a full generation since the realm had been at peace and the two sovereigns, who succeeded the Lancastrians, had been the brothers Edward IV, who died in 1483, and Richard III.

The House of York, to whom the White Rose has been given as a symbol, as a grouping showed energy, vigour and intelligence; they were not trustworthy. Edward III had created the first English dukedoms and they represented in the male line his fourth son the Duke of York and as heirs general his second son the Duke of Clarence. Their own male heirs were disappearing. The two sons of Edward IV had been murdered and the only son of Richard III had died. But one of the factors of the reign of Henry VII and his son is the presence of the blood of the White Rose.

When the Earl of Richmond's landing had been completed, and Richard III had been defeated and killed at Bosworth Field, the members of the rival house were nearly all minors. The younger daughters of Edward IV were between thirteen and five years of age, the daughter and son of his brother the Duke of Clarence were twelve and ten. The one exception was John de la Pole Earl of Lincoln, the son of Edward IV's sister Elizabeth, who was just twenty. These and their descendants would cause anxiety to the House of Tudor for close on sixty years.

There is another factor in the situation: Richard III had impugned the marriage of his elder brother with Elizabeth Woodville, asserting that Edward IV had been pre-contracted to Lady Eleanor Butler, the Earl of Shrewsbury's widowed daughter. Henry VII was quick and sensitive and not without a vein of superstition. It seems to me that this last charge did something to tarnish for him the claims of the Princess Elizabeth.

In addition to this inherent weakness in the position of the Tudor family, there was a difficulty arising from the massive legitimacy of the rival stocks. For various reasons the great bastards who flourished in France and Burgundy in the previous century, had no counterpart in English life. In some ways these men of whom the *Bâtard* de Dunois is, perhaps, the best-known example, were of real service to the stocks they served. Whatever their power, they had no claim to the succession of the royal and ducal families from which they sprang.

Similarly there is little record of mistresses in the lives of the Kings of England in the fifteenth century with the exception of Jane Shore, who was the mistress of Edward IV for the greater part of his reign; but there is in any case no record throughout these years of an accepted royal bastard. Marital fidelity also marked the women of the great families. The position was made easier by their marked fertility and by the careful seclusion of their lives. All these factors tended to build up the survival but not the resilience of the old great families.

There were two other stocks who to their misfortune had claims as heirs general to members of the old royal line. Edward Stafford, third Duke of Buckingham was seven years of age at the time of Bosworth and his father had been killed by Richard III after an unsuccessful effort on Richmond's behalf. He was the heir general of the Duke of Gloucester, the youngest son of Edward III. The Staffords were an unlucky family with rashness and small intelligence. None of the three dukes died in their beds.

The last 'claimant' family the House of Howard had inherited the rights of the Mowbrays Dukes of Norfolk, but at the beginning of the reign were in a very weak position. Both these titles Norfolk and Buckingham had been in use by the old royal family. It was a misfortune to inherit them.

There were also the Courtenays Earls of Devon and the Greys Marquesses of Dorset, the first married into the blood royal, while the second was related to the King. The heads of both these houses had supported King Henry at Bosworth and had died during his reign. The new Earl of Devon had been born in 1475 and married when twenty years of age the Lady Katharine, who was the only one of the younger daughters of Edward IV who married and left issue. His family later suffered the disasters that came to those who had these royal descents. The second Marquess of Dorset was born in 1478; he bore a title which had been held by the Beauforts and his father had been a stepson of Edward IV. Unlike all the other stocks that have been mentioned the Greys were without any *claim* to the throne; this family passed quite peacefully through the first two Tudor reigns.

Under Henry VII Clarence's daughter the Lady Margaret was married to Sir Richard Pole, one of that King's early supporters and a kinsman. The Staffords, Courtenays and Poles were the core of the old-fashioned nobility, the over-spill of the fifteenth century.

II

The House of Dorset

There was one great family who, although they were related closely to Henry VIII were in their approach quite different from these ancient stocks. The second Marquess of Dorset was in fact the King's first cousin for his father had been the elder stepbrother to the King's mother; but there was never any element of jealousy in the relationship; he was not in succession to the Crown.

Thomas Grey, who had inherited the Dorset marquessate in 1501, was considerably older than his sovereign, a man of thirty-two at his accession. He was a skilled jouster; five foot eight inches in height and with smooth yellow hair.[1] All his life he had been about the Court, made a Knight of the Bath at seventeen and receiving the Garter soon after he came of age. His mother Cecil, 'the old Lady Marquess', had brought him estates in the West Country as the heiress-general of the Bonvilles. He himself had married Margaret daughter of Sir Robert Wotton of Boughton Malherbe, the head of a Kentish stock which would become an official family in the Elizabethan period. He was constantly in his master's company, an intimate of long standing. In 1523 he was a gentleman of the privy chamber, not a high place for one of his great rank.

The two great ministers of the reign both began their rise through the Grey family. The Marquess's three young brothers had been placed at Magdalen College School under the care of Dr Wolsey, to whom their father had given his first benefice, the rectory of Limington in Somerset. Thomas Cromwell, as a young lawyer had been appointed manager of the affairs of the old Lady Marquess. The family was alive to all their opportunities. After all

---

[1] His body was found intact when his coffin in the collegiate church at Astley in Warwickshire was opened in 1608.

Dorset was to be the grandfather of Lady Jane Grey, the nine days' Queen.

With the exception of the unsuccessful leadership of a single military expedition the Marquesses of Dorset had no part in administrative life. The family offered the successive Kings their gift of friendship. They went with the times quite easily; they were like those great French houses which were in tune with the modern age and thus open to Calvinism. Like so many other men of moderate ability, they went where their King might choose to lead them.

Henry VIII had that contented vanity which comes to the young athlete who is more successful at his virile exercises than those about him. He was a better shot than the archers of his guard. It was a happiness to hear their praise come back to him.

He was not one of those Kings who search out for able ministers; he took what was at hand for him and thus found Wolsey.

Wolsey was energetic and deeply acquisitive. He was only thirty-four at King Henry's accession. It was soon evident that he was a perfect servant. He became one of the royal chaplains in 1507, recommended to Henry VII by Sir Richard Nanfan, the Deputy of Calais, whom he had served in many ways. Henry VIII sent him on diplomatic missions and Wolsey accumulated benefices including the parish of Redgrave from the Abbot of Bury St Edmund's and that of Lydd from the Abbot of Tintern. He was prebendary of Stow Longa in Lincoln Cathedral and soon gained another prebend in Hereford. He was given the great parish of Torrington. He must have become known very early to spread his gains in this way across England. Shortly before the King's accession he was promoted to the deanery of Lincoln. His rise thereafter was quite steady, and in 1511 he became a privy councillor and Registrar of the Order of the Garter; he was henceforward a member of the King's court.

A careful examination of a very familiar source, Hall's *Chronicles*, with a fresh eye, will give us various side-lights upon the reign. It was on New Year's Day 1511 that the Queen gave birth to a son, who was christened Henry and created Prince of Wales. The God-parents were the Archbishop of Canterbury and the Earl of Surrey, later the second Duke of Norfolk, and Katharine Countess of Devonshire. The account of the joust on this occasion is worth recalling, so many figures of the reign are now revealed. 'Shortly after and before the Queen's churching', wrote Edward Hall,[1] 'the King rode to Walsingham. The Queen being churched and puri-fied, the King and she removed from Richmond to Westminster, where was preparation for a solemn joust in honour of the Queen, the King being one and with him three aides: His Grace being called *Cure Loial*, the Lord William, Earl of Devonshire called *Bon Voloir*, Sir Thomas Knevet called *Bon Espoir*, Sir Edward Neville called *Valiaunt desire*, they four to run at the tilt against all comers.' These details suggest the names of the King's intimates in these first days.

'A place[2] in the palace was prepared for the King, and also the Queen . . . the innerpart [decorated] with cloth of gold, and the outer with rich cloth of Arras.' There was a pageant 'of great quantity' made like a forest with a castle standing made of gold and before the castle gate sat a gentleman fresh apparelled making a garland of roses. This forest was drawn as it were by the strength of two great beasts, a Lion and an Antelope. 'The Lion flourished all over with Damaske gold, the Antelope wrought all over with silver of Damaske.'

The next day there was more elaboration. 'Then came the King[3] under a pavilion of cloth of gold and purple velvet em-broidered and powdered H and K [for Henry and Katharine] of fine gold, the compass of the pavilion above embroidered richly and valenced with flat gold. Then on the counter-part entred Sir Charles Brandon. Then came the Marques Dorset and Sir Thomas Boleyn, like two pilgrims from St James [of Compostella] in tabards of black velvet.' After supper, 'His grace with the Queen, Lords and Ladies came into the White Hall, within the said palace, which was hanged richly, the hall was scaffolded and railed on all parts. There was an interlude of the Gentlemen of his Chapel before His Grace and divers fresh songs.'

On the first of May the King was in his palace at Greenwich beside the river. In the jousts he was supported by Sir Edward Howard, Sir Charles Brandon and Sir Edward Neville in 'coats of green satin guarded with crimson velvet' and on the other side the

---

[1] Edward Hall, *Henry VIII*, edition of 1904, p. 22.
[2] *ibid.*, p. 23.   [3] *ibid.*, pp. 24, 25.

Earls of Essex and Devonshire, the Marquess of Dorset and Lord Howard were all 'in crimson satin guarded with a "pounced" setting of green velvet'. On the third day the Queen made a great banquet to the King and to all those who had jousted. After the banquet Her Grace gave the chief prize to the King, the second to the Earl of Essex, the third to the Earl of Devonshire and the fourth to the Lord Marquess of Dorset.

Before these ceremonies were all completed there had come misfortune. 'The young Prince, which was born on New Years day, upon the two and twentieth day of February, being then the eve of St Mathias, departed this world at Richmond.'[1] It was the beginning of the end of all the happiness of H and K and it would be a quarter of a century before the King received the gift of another son born as a prince.

Hall was a lawyer, who had a deep interest in the art of spectacle. So long as he is describing material there is no reason to suppose that he is anything but absolutely accurate. He is dealing with that unsubstantial world which was to have its final flowering at the Field of the Cloth of Gold. The stress which is always put on gold is very curious, for these were the generations before the great cargoes of gold were sailed in from the Indies. The roof of the Roman basilica of Santa Maria Maggiore is an example of what was done with this new metal. But King Henry's gold was for the most part not metal, it was silks and gold thread and similar materials, the confections of imagined castles, gold paint and wood. Before the actual gold in buildings was as yet envisaged, there was an elaborate gold stitch to serve a prince's vanity. This was a reign of heavy built-up dress against a transitory backcloth.

There is also a point to be made about the King's companions. In the early days there were very few 'new men', churchmen always excluded, about the King. The royal companions mentioned were of the old world, the Courtenays and their first cousin Henry Bourchier Earl of Essex,[2] the Nevilles and the Howards and the latter's relatives the Knyvetts. And there were always present Dorset and his brothers Lord Leonard Grey and Lord Anthony,

---

[1] Hall, *Henry VIII*, p. 27.
[2] While he shared a descent from the Duke of Gloucester, Lord Essex (b. 1472, d. 1540) was also a nephew of Queen Elizabeth (Woodville).

and even in these early years Sir Charles Brandon and Sir Thomas Boleyn. The latter was in fact a son-in-law of the second Duke of Norfolk. Without exception they had all come down from Henry VII's Court.

One subject alone appears to have been too grand to take a part in these proceedings, Edward Stafford Duke of Buckingham. These earliest companions were for the most part in some way related to the King. In the first years of his reign he was most kind to the 'White Rose' families and, perhaps, the influence of the Queen may be traced here. She had left Spain when she was a child; but during her lonely life in England after her widowhood she was much under the influence of Doña Elvira Manuel, her duenna, and Don Pedro Manrique, her major domo. Her Castilian mind would have approved of the high blood of those by whom her young husband was now surrounded. While most of the great families of the first part of the reign had a certain natural sympathy for the Queen, there was one which remained cold at heart towards her, the Howard complex.

The situation at an old authoritarian Court was never static, there was always a family or a group of families, which was rising to a position of greater power. At this period it was the House of Howard. Their high position was unusual for in the male line they were merely the representatives of a family of small East Anglian landowners. Sir Robert Howard of Tendring, a vanished manor in the valley of the Stour on the Suffolk–Essex borders, had married in the reign of Henry IV the elder daughter of the first Duke of Norfolk of the Mowbray line. To make the disparity less great the family were at that time out of favour and the dukedom under attainder. The Mowbray line was re-instated and continued until 1483. In that year Lord Howard was created Duke of Norfolk and Earl Marshal of England. He was, as has been said, through his mother, the Mowbray heiress, the representative and heir general of Margaret Duchess of Norfolk, the only child of Thomas of Brotherton, younger son of Edward I.

The first Duke of Norfolk of the Howard line had been killed at Bosworth field beside his master and his son Surrey had been wounded in that battle. It was in these years that Surrey, as the victor in the battle of Flodden against the Scots, was restored to

1 Francis I

The Lord Vaux.

2 Thomas, Lord Vaux

the dukedom and received for life the office of Earl Marshal. The second Duke was an old man now, just on seventy, and belonged therefore to the reign rather than to King Henry's personal life. Inevitably he died before the coming of the religious changes. The third Duke, who will be considered later, was one of the great figures of the new King's reign. There was nothing inbred about the Howards. Most of their ancestry came from among the squirearchy of East Anglia. Norfolk had a single quality, which was very rare among the great men around him, a tireless and an unsleeping vigilance.

In their last days both Henry VII and his mother were preoccupied with plans for building what is now the Henry VII chapel in Westminster Abbey. Three new monks were[1] to be added to the foundation for the purpose of saying weekly Masses in this chapel; they had either to be bachelors or doctors of divinity from Oxford or Cambridge. On the King's anniversary every monk in the house was expected to say a Mass of Requiem. Fees were to be given 'to the lords chancellor and treasurer, to the chiefs of the law, to the lord mayor, the recorder and sheriffs of London' provided that they attended these celebrations.

There is evidence that the royal family and the new young King were much more religious, in the sense of a taste for liturgical observance, than were the majority of his subjects. Henry VIII had a taste for liturgy, considered as a concomitant of kingship; this was a taste which neither of his great ministers not Cardinal Wolsey and certainly not Thomas Cromwell would ever share.

[1] *A House of Kings, the Official History of Westminster Abbey* (1966), p. 96.

c

III

The Cloth of Gold

In the early years of the reign the old practitioners of kingship, Ferdinand of Aragon and the Emperor Maximilian were still alive. Louis XII of France, a rather younger man, had been brought up by his father-in-law Louis XI. Pope Julius II, who was in himself the chief opponent of the Borgia Papacy, was still reigning. Within quite a short time these survivors from the policies of the fifteenth century would pass away. A firm nationalism was now established in the countries of Western Europe. Ferdinand seized Spanish Navarre and the Pyrenees was henceforward a political, as it had long been a national, frontier. It was this national character of France which would have rendered useless King Henry's early projects to reconquer the former possessions of his Crown in Aquitaine.

These years also saw the building up of Wolsey's great position. From 1511 he had been a privy councillor and he had helped the King in his first war with France and still more with the peace which followed this in 1513. As an organizer he had great capacity and he had that taste for luxury and for extravagance, which the young King valued in one who so soon became his own chief servant. He gained from the Pope the diocese of Therouanne, but not the entry to that see. From the accession of Francis I of France on New Year's Day 1515 he became the more or less permanent adviser of a peace with France. His ecclesiastical career was moving forward. At the beginning of 1514 he received the bishopric of Lincoln and in that winter the archbishopric of York. In September of the next year Pope Leo X created him Cardinal priest of the title of Santa Cecilia in *Trastevere* and three months later the King gave him the Lord Chancellorship. Henceforward, until his destruction, he was all in all.

It must be stressed that in this halcyon period of the reign Wolsey's promotion caused his master but little trouble. The then Archbishop of Canterbury, William Warham, had readily surrendered the chancellorship and Wolsey was the chief *protégé* of Richard Foxe, the old Bishop of Winchester, who had been the leading ecclesiastical statesman of the old King's reign. And then Wolsey had a daemonic energy which separated him from contemporary churchmen, and his tastes were modern. In the early days the King could not but admire the great pile that Wolsey was erecting at Hampton Court.

There were so many elements which his sovereign would appreciate, his work of administration as that field was then considered, his capacity to set forth an army, his powers which he had already exercised as an ambassador. This was the last period at which a cardinal was received as a prince of the Holy Roman Church in all the often warring countries of Western and Central Europe. Wolsey seems to have paid attention to the career of Cardinal d'Amboise, the great politico-religious figure of the reign of Louis XII, and he shared with him a transient interest in the possibility of succeeding to the Papal throne. He approached religious display from the side of splendour; his claim to have his cross carried before him in the province of Canterbury as well as in that of York; the various appurtenances of his later state as cardinal legate. He was deeply concerned with cardinalitial ceremonial seen as a pendant to the King's own ceremonies. Liturgy, considered by itself, had left him cold.

The Cardinal of York, a diocese he never visited until his political disaster, had therefore no influence on the religious side of the King's character, nor on that of the Queen or on the members of the ancient stocks. It was essentially on the secular side of the King's policies that he acted on him. And it is a difficult matter for any minister to fascinate a sovereign by a combination of ability with luxury and splendour. This is sometimes practicable where there is an emotional attachment; but there was no emotional attachment here. There was here nothing which could shield a minister when he came in time to wake the King's unslumbering jealousy.

In the last century before the Reformation the Cardinals who were ministers of sovereign princes had attained to a great international position. They had relations with the royal houses to which their predecessors had not attained. Thus Wolsey would write with respectful intimacy to the Countess of Angoulême, the French King's mother, and with Francis I he would maintain close correspondence, which would only be interrupted during those months when the kings of France and England might be at war. For himself Wolsey was always polarized towards the French alliance, the only possible combination which might perhaps bring him to the Papal throne.

It has never seemed to me that his personal origin was of significance. He came from Ipswich from that established middle class whose wealth was then increasing. The fact that his father is termed a butcher does not give an adequate impression of his solid background; but in any case the clergy or to be more precise those priests who had come out from the universities and were now engaged in part in diplomacy or in the civil service formed a markedly egalitarian society. At the other end of the scale the same condition held. Among the members of the Sacred College it was only those who came from almost princely families like Cardinal Beaufort or Cardinal Bourchier in the fifteenth century and Reginald Cardinal Pole, who lived at the end of Catholic rule in England, who stood apart. Cardinal Wolsey was the last of the chief ministers of England, who had the possibility of a later life in a great position upon the Continent.

There are several angles from which the Field of the Cloth of Gold can be examined. In the first place this was the only occasion on which the whole of the English Court was brought across the Channel. In its setting it was the last act of the world of Froissart, and it carried on from the time of the Hundred Years War the example of an, at-heart, unfriendly rivalry with the King of France. But the English Court involved was something which had developed since the fifteenth century. The setting was of the first period of the reign; it would become unimaginable in later years. It had all the canvas and the painted wood which would seem unbelievably old-fashioned to the Elizabethans. There was also an emphasis, unique in modern English history, on the physical attributes of the sovereign. In England it had in many ways the effect

of an army called up for an invasion. It was an exercise of the
Cardinal's capacity for construction.

The voyage from Dover to Calais was at that time between two
ports both owing allegiance to the English Crown. In fact Calais
was throughout the reign in the King's mind; it was the English
fortress against the southern enemy as Berwick was against the
northern. The transport of the Court to the Field of the Cloth of
Gold was one of the responsibilities of the Royal Navy, the operation was under the immediate control of Sir William Fitzwilliam,
then Vice-Admiral of England.

The office of Lord High Admiral of England ante-dated by
some generations the establishment of a true naval service. It was
one of the great offices of State parallel to that of the Admirals of
France and Castile. It implied in very general terms command of
the royal forces when these were embarked to fight upon the sea.
The gentlemen who embarked on these occasions had hitherto
only seen service on land. On one occasion only, the Lord Admiral
of England was killed in action.

In 1513 the second Duke of Norfolk's second son Sir Edward
Howard was slain in an attack on the French galleys under Pré-
gent de Bidoux at Blancs Sablons. In a will Sir Edward asked the
King to choose one of his bastard sons for his bodyguard and to
this son he bequeathed his barque *Genett*. To the other, because he
had no ship, he left c marks and asked Sir Charles Brandon to set
him forward in the world. To Sir Charles he left his 'rope of gold
nobles that I hang my great whistle by' and the great whistle, his
sign of office, he bequeathed to the King's noble Grace. For the
time being the Earl of Surrey held his younger brother's post.

The ships took their part in the act of spectacle. The largest of
the royal vessels was the *Henry Grace à Dieu* and others were named
for the Queen and the King's sister, the *Katherine Fortaleza* and the
small ships the *Katherine Pleasaunce* and the *Katherine*[1] galley, and
then the *Mary George*, the *Mary Rose* and the *Mary Gloria*. The
Henry Grace à Dieu, of which fairly exact details are now known,
was built at Erith in 1518 and the others joined the Navy in the
first nine years of the reign.

[1] From this period there was another naval vessel with the same name, the *Katherine
Pomegranate*.

The large picture entitled 'The Embarkation of Henry VIII at Dover, May 31st, 1528' now hangs in the National Maritime Museum. As in so many pictures of the time the name of Holbein was associated with it and it was for long attributed erroneously to Vincenzo Vulpe. It is now accepted as probably derived from the Low Countries and its painter as unknown.[1] A careful study shows that at any rate it was not contemporary. It is clearly intended as a glorification and not a record. Laird Clowes states[2] that Dover harbour was not deep enough to admit the ships represented as emerging from that port. It seems that the ships in the picture include, besides the *Henry Grace à Dieu*, the *Sovereign*, *Gabriel Royal*, *Mary Rose* and *Katherine Fortaleza*. There is no reason to suppose that these were present on this occasion.

The actual detail of the ships themselves appears correct. The King himself is represented in the waist of the flagship. He is wearing a garment of cloth of gold, edged with ermine, the sleeves, jacket and breeches crimson. His hat bears a white feather lying along the brim. He is surrounded by certain courtiers, the one beside him wearing a dark violet coat, slashed with black and with red stockings.[3] Behind them are the yeomen of the guard with halberds. Two trumpeters are seated on the break of the poop and two more on the break of the forecastle, all four are carrying their trumpets. The royal arms, party per pale Argent and Vert, within the garter, the arms of England and France quarterly crowned are displayed at the stern and at the break of the forecastle. A boat at her stern is flying the banner of St George. The ships are all wearing long pendants which fly outwards in the light airs. In the background is Dover Castle with two small towers immediately in the foreground. It is a crowded, indeed an overcrowded scene. Quite apart from the accuracy of presentation, it was the kind of painting that was valued in the King's reign.

These royal ships appear again and again throughout this period. They were laid up in harbour every winter, their lives were long. There seems to have been no new building. That well-known ship the *Jesus of Lubeck* was obtained from the Hanseatic League

---

[1] Cf. Ellis Waterhouse, *Painting in Britain, 1530–1790* (1953), p. 4.
[2] *The Royal Navy, a History* (1897), vol. i, p. 406.
[3] *ibid.*, i, pp. 407–8.

some time later in this reign. There is reference to an inquiry[1] from the King of Denmark's chancellor as to whether King Henry might like to purchase the *Great Mary* from the Danish Navy. It does not seem that this offer was taken up. There is a reference[2] to the *Great Spaniard*, which was a gift to King Henry from the Emperor; but there is no further mention of her. There is a note[3] as to the cost of rigging and caulking the *Mary Glory* at Deptford Strand.

There are three comments on the King's crossing to France. John Hope, clerk of the King's ships, noted[4] that the *Mary Rose* and two other royal ships, the *Great Bark* and *Little Bark*, as well as two smaller vessels, were ordered to scour the seas, while the passengers were crossing. The Warden of the Cinque Ports had been instructed[5] to make ready ships and hoys. As to the actual voyage there is a statement[6] from the Venetian Ambassador that the King and the Queen and the Court quitted Dover with twenty-seven ships and arrived at Calais at noon after a very calm passage.

Meanwhile there was another question which affected the King's plans for this French meeting. Charles V, the Emperor-Elect, was about to return by sea to the Low Countries, but his ships were held up at Corunna by the persistence of winds from the north-east. He could not in fact leave until a very few days before the King was due to cross to France. The English Court had in fact gone down to Canterbury to prepare for its embarkation. As the Spanish ships were sailing up the Channel, the Cardinal was sent to welcome the Emperor at Dover. The next morning the King arrived to bring him to Canterbury. An account[7] of this ceremony has survived.

At the reception of the Emperor at Canterbury Cathedral, King Henry and his guest entered at the principal door and walked along a carpet of purple velvet to the kneeling desk covered with gold brocade and furnished with two gold cushions. They then moved forward under a canopy of cloth of gold to the High altar

[1] *Letters and Papers, Foreign and Domestic, 1524–6*, p. 4.
[2] *ibid.*, p. 119.
[3] *Letters and Papers, Foreign and Domestic, 1519–21*, p. 343.
[4] *ibid.*, p. 240.   [5] *ibid.*, p. 239.
[6] *Calendar of State Papers, Venetian, 1520–6*, ed. Rawdon Brown (1864–), p. 15.
[7] *Cal. S.P. Venetian, 1520–6*, pp. 13–18.

where the Archbishop intoned the *Veni Creator Spiritus* for it was Whit Sunday.

In Canterbury there were sixty dappled palfreys prepared for the coming of Germaine Queen of Aragon, now married to the Margrave John of Brandenburg. Queen Germaine, a daughter of the Count of Foix, was the widow of the Emperor's grandfather Ferdinand of Aragon, whom she had married after the death of Isabella of Castile.

Afterwards going past twenty of the Queen of England's pages in gold brocade and crimson satin in chequers the sovereigns ascended fifteen steps of a marble staircase and then on the landing found the Queen of England, dressed in cloth of gold lined with ermine. There were strings of beautiful pearls about her neck. The Cardinal stood beside her, wearing a cape of crimson camlet lined with ermine.

Their majesties dined alone, the King and Queen and Lady Mary his sister and the Emperor. The Duke of Suffolk brought in a large gold basin with a cover bearing a crane. In the centre stood a small gold cup. The Margrave of Brandenburg's brother took off the cover. Water was poured over the sovereigns' fingers; the brother of the Count Palatine of the Rhine presented the towel; the basin was removed by the Duke of Buckingham. A second gold basin was brought in by the Earl of Northumberland's eldest son; the Marquess of Dorset uncovered it; the towel was presented by the old Duke of Norfolk.

Queen Germaine made her entry accompanied by sixty ladies on horseback, mounted on white palfreys, saddled with cloth of gold. In the Emperor's company was the Prince of Orange,[1] a youth about eighteen years of age. His entire costume, doublet, shoes and hose was of silver lamé striped longitudinally with cloth of gold.

On the Tuesday evening the Emperor left Canterbury and was accompanied by the King for the first five miles of his journey. The Cardinal, who was clad throughout in crimson, with his horse apparelled in the same colour, went with him to the coast at Sandwich, where the Spanish vessels were now lying. The party

---

[1] This was Philibert, Prince of Orange (b. 1502, d. 1530), the last ruler of the House of Chalon.

moved eastward through the mid-summer night across the
Kentish countryside, the bodyguard carrying long wax candles of
the English fashion.

Something in these ceremonies struck the Duke of Buckingham
as menial. The colours mentioned are nearly all sharp and simple,
the crimson and the white and silver and the ermine and, above
all, the gold. Very much of these processions was an exercise in
heraldry.

Time and again there are references to Wolsey and this was
only just for the whole arrangement for the Field of the Cloth of
Gold was in his hands. He had a talent for organization which
at that date was quite extraordinary. It was exactly the kind of
scene the King required. He was still brave and lazy; there was
as yet nothing to arouse his jealousy. He took complacently all
those good things that his remarkable servant now set before
him.

The plans for transporting the Court were going forward. A
feature of the temporary palace which had been constructed at
Guines was a large chapel entirely covered and hung with cloth of
gold and green velvet. Statues of the twelve apostles in gold and a
great crucifix stood on the altar. Arrangements had to be made for
five princes of the church, for in addition to the Cardinal of York
there were four Cardinals of France. Among those accompanying
the King were the Deans of the Chapel Royal and St Paul's. The
rich copes and vestments given to Westminster Abbey by the late
King were to be borrowed for the voyage. At Calais the church of
St Nicholas was to be temporarily the Chapel Royal. The seats
were all to be removed and a gallery made between the church and
the King's lodging. The clerk of the closet was to warn the chaplains who accompanied the King to provide the closet with the
best hangings, travers, jewels, images and altar cloths that the
King had.

The number of priests present was immense. There were eleven
priests belonging to the Chapel Royal and six provided for the
Queen's arrangements. The Cardinal and the Archbishop of
Canterbury brought between them seventeen chaplains and the
seven bishops another twenty-eight. This is understandable, it is
the number of those who were in attendance on the laymen that is

surprising. Thus the Dukes of Buckingham and Suffolk had four chaplains each. Even assuming that some of the peers and knights left their chaplains behind them, it seemed that there were present at the Field of the Cloth of Gold well over two hundred priests.[1]

The general arrangements for the meeting on the English side were in the hands of the Lord Chamberlain the Earl of Worcester and the Lord Privy Seal the Bishop of Durham. They were survivors of the old Court and both were soon to die – in 1526 and 1523. Charles Somerset had had an interesting career. The date of his birth is doubtful, 1460 is suggested, and very little is known about his childhood. He had nothing in common with the White Rose families; he was indeed the one sprig of the Red Rose. He was the only natural child of the last of the Beaufort Dukes of Somerset. It seems that in his boyhood he was cared for by his cousin, the Lady Margaret, Henry VII's mother.

Everything had to be provided for him, estates confiscated from the Yorkist families, a career at Court, a wealthy marriage. The King bestowed on him Lady Elizabeth Herbert the orphan heiress of the last Earl of Pembroke of the first creation. From the last days of the old King he had been chamberlain of the household. Henry VIII followed, as so often, in his father's footsteps. Somerset was sent to France on many negotiations and in 1514 he was created Earl of Worcester. His great estates lay in the West of England. His principal holdings came from his wife's inheritance and were based on Raglan Castle.

Alone among the sovereigns of his royal house, King Henry took delight in building up the fortunes of his 'creatures'. Another example is the Duke of Suffolk, whose case will be examined later. There was a common factor in these peers. There was no danger that they might outstrip their sovereign in intelligence.

The same close concern was accorded to those ecclesiastics who were in effect employed in what could be considered as the Crown's foreign service. For them as for those in high civil employ-

---

[1] The figures can be deduced from those given from the list in Bodleian MS; Ashmole 1115, ff. 95–9 printed in Dr J. G. Russell's admirable study *The Field of the Cloth of Gold* (1969), pp. 191–204. There were supposed to be present forty chaplains for the greater peers and forty-four for the barons and one hundred and seven for the Knights and esquires of the King's party. The laymen of the Queen's party were to be attended by another thirty-six.

ment, it was the King for whom they worked and by the King they were rewarded with offices of Church and State.

Like Lord Worcester, Thomas Rushall the Bishop of Durham also belonged to a passing generation. While still a protonotary Henry VII sent him on an embassy to France in 1499 and he had subsequently held the post of royal secretary. He was appointed Bishop of Durham by the dying sovereign; King Henry VIII made him Lord Privy Seal. The great chamber at Bishop Auckland is his legacy. Worcester and the Bishop of Durham were typical of the first generation of the new King's royal servants. Both men had taken the Cardinal's rise to power quite tranquilly.

The organizers of the expedition belonged very much to the old world. The oversight for the arrangements as to who should accompany the King to France was entrusted to the Earl of Essex and Lord Abergavenny. The selection of those from Devonshire were in the hands of Lord Fitzwarine and from Westmorland in Sir Thomas Parr's. There were no representatives from Cornwall, or from the two northern English counties. No arrangements were made for Wales and there seem to have been no gentlemen from the principality at the Field of the Cloth of Gold and very few from the lands beyond the Severn. In fact among all the courtiers present the only Welsh name found is that of Sir Griffith Rhys and he is described in the list as coming from Worcestershire. The absence of the whole body of the Welsh and Cornish gentry is very striking.

There is a note[1] of conduct money for a party riding down to Dover and composed of a captain, a petty captain, chaplain, fifes, drums and archers. In regard to the dress stuffs and the food[2] there were purchases for the Queen of white satin, green satin of Bruges and yellow satin, of green velvet, yellow and russet velvet, of blue sarcenet and silver damask and white cloth of gold. There was broad grey cloth, and grey, white and scarlet kersey for her male attendants. There were fifty russet and green horse cloths lined with canvas, and ten yards of violet satin for lining a vallance of cloth of gold. There were five spruce chests with hanging locks and one thousand feet of glass from St Omer.

A special price was given to the King's sea fisher for five dories,

[1] ibid., p. 299.   [2] ibid., p. 296.

and a purchase of nine thousand plaice and seven thousand whiting. There were partridges, lapwings and pigeon. Thomas Woodroffe was paid for thirteen swans. The mayor of Dover supervised the carriage of seventeen bucks from Essex to Guines. A gift of venison was sent to Calais by the Earl of Arundel.

It was a blazing summer. The Court of England and its retainers and all the provisions to sustain them were quietly ferried over the smooth seas to what was then still English soil, the Pale of Calais.

IV

The Palace at Guines

Various aspects of the great gathering are striking. In the first place it was remarkably old-fashioned and it is hard for us to believe that it took place in the same century which saw the reigns of Queen Elizabeth and of Catherine de Medicis and the last Valois kings. In many of its aspects it belonged rather to the period of Charles the Bold and the dishes and arrangements of the Court of Burgundy. There was, for instance, great play with sugar and culinary subtleties.[1]

At the same time Wolsey was an old-fashioned Cardinal and perhaps this was the last occasion for the display of mediaeval heraldry. He was accompanied by fifty gentlemen of his household, bare-headed and in crimson velvet with massive golden chains about their necks. There were fifty gentlemen ushers bearing gold maces. He had two riding chaplains bearing crosses. All these were clad in crimson. There was the cardinalitial mule caparisoned in red and gold. The two silver pillars were carried before him as were the two silver pole-axes. The Cardinal himself, riding his mule and wearing a robe of crimson figured velvet, wore his great hat with tassels on this occasion.

On the heraldic side there were the Cardinal's arms, the sable shield and engrailed cross of the Ufford Earls of Suffolk and the azure leopards' faces of the de la Poles, the rose of Lancaster and the choughs reputed to be the arms of St Thomas of Canterbury, Wolsey's patron.

The Kings of arms from both countries were present as were such heraldic officers as some of the great families still maintained.

---

[1] Cf. for a detailed description, *The Field of the Cloth of Gold*, p. 87.

There was a sense that all gentlemen of coat armour were born equal. Thus in the competitions, Francis Brian, a simple esquire, made one of the top scores in broken lances. Orleans and Clarencieux kings of arms proclaimed the heraldic bearings of all contestants. This, too, was something that belonged essentially to the earlier centuries.

In fact everything connected with the tournament seemed to belong to a dying world. There were the fifteen hundred spear staves from the armoury at the Tower; the mill for the royal armoury brought across to Guines from Greenwich with the mill horses; the forges that were set up there. Only the thousand swords from Milan would outlast this transient scene.

Curiously enough it is the movement of the horses which best suggests the rudimentary trade routes of that time. There were the Spanish jennets which the Emperor had brought from their home country and the coursers of Naples, which were favourites at the English Court. There was the bay courser bred by the Duke of Termoli, which the King rode. He was bred in the neighbourhood of that little town in the now-forgotten diocese of Termoli and Guardialfiera to the north of Manfredonia on the Adriatic Sea. The King of France's came from the Gonzaga stud at Mantua in Lombardy.

Figures given a few years later, in 1532, describe the town of Calais as then containing 2,400 beds and stabling for 2,000 horses. This town was probably the headquarters of the great body of the English contingent consisting of thirty-four peers and nineteen peeresses, and 132 knights, eighteen accompanied by their wives. There were also twenty-four maids of honour. It had an element of the family party, Sir Robert and Sir Anthony Poyntz and, among the maids of honour, the latter's daughters. The King and Queen and his sister the Duchess of Suffolk lay in the palace at Guines, almost eight miles away.

The palace was a strictly temporary affair, a confected castle, and it lay to the southwards of that country town.[1] It was on the elevated land of the Pas de Calais where the roads ran eastwards into Flanders. The sun beat down upon it, as hot as a Roman

[1] Cf. for details and discussions about this building, *The Field of the Cloth of Gold*, pp. 35–41.

summer, wrote an Italian commentator. From away to the westward came the breezes from the sea. The palace was built of brick
on a stone foundation up to the height of eight feet. The further
thirty feet was made of timber painted to resemble brick. The roof
of seared canvas was intended to suggest slate. There were stone
chimneys. The great entrance gate was surmounted by Tudor
roses and over these was placed a semi-circular scalloped arch
above the roof line. Within there was, principally, a great dining
hall and a chapel. The greatest novelty were the panes of diamond
glass in the eight windows. Everything was transitory about the
palace. The summer sunshine was very kind to it. The palace was
soon taken down and no surviving painting is contemporary.
Away to the south on the French border lay the golden valley
where the tournaments took place and further on at Ardres the
forest of great tents which sheltered the French Court.

There are episodes which illuminate the whole of one aspect of
that generation's knowledge. Thus on one occasion when King
Henry left his palace he was accompanied by the three Worthies,
Julius Caesar and Hector and Alexander, and by the three Princes
of Jewry, David, Joshua and Julius Maccabeus, the last three having masks whose beards were formed of fine gold thread. And then
there came the three Christian princes, Charlemagne, Arthur and
Godfrey of Bouillon. This very well preserved their view of history.
It was of course the historiography of England, not of the Continent. It was very English like the white thorn emblem which the
King displayed as a reminder of the finding of King Richard's
crown beneath the hawthorn bush on Bosworth field.

The wines at the banquets included those Greek and Spanish
wines which had been long popular in England. They were
sweet and sugar sweetened them still further, Malmsey from
Momemvasia and at this date imported from the Cretan vineyards,
Romania or Romeyn imported from the Ionian Islands, Canary
wine, Madeira, Muscadel. The term Rhenish wine then covered
the German imports. These were paralleled by the French vin-
tages. After all France had been for many centuries a wine-drink-
ing nation and London was the most northern of those capitals
where wine flowed in the channels of the streets on State occasions.
We can sense that the French wines were making headway and it

was in fact the sweet French wine of Anjou, 'which old King Henry loved', that was crystallized in sixteenth-century legend.

In considering the arrangements for the royal meeting one obtains the impression that the King of England accepted all that was put before him. He had that clear and deep concern for field sports and for liturgy which went with a character that was ultimately philistine. It has not been an uncommon combination among the upper classes of the Old Religion. He was determined to display his skill at archery. So much was built up for his satisfaction. He was at this time young and cubbish, but he was a tiger cub.

Francis I was very different. He lacked his English rival's strain of gaiety. He was a well-built man,[1] superbly dressed with a thick and neat black beard, the whole face dominated by the huge nose and by his careful eyes. His ruling passion was the thought of Italy. For three generations now the Kings of France had been beguiled by the claims of the House of Valois and its predecessors to the duchy of Milan. Such a desire made opposition from the Emperor a certainty. It was thus most important that the northern French frontier should be secured against attack from England. Francis I probably had much less interest in the actual details of the royal meeting than had King Henry. He certainly spent much less money on the preparations and the French display was confined to the great tents which were clearly much less expensive than the confections of the English castle.

The Cardinal kept throughout his years of power a strong self-interested sympathy for France and a close relation with the French King's mother. It has recently been suggested[2] that Wolsey did not want the papal throne. In fact it seems to me that the prospect always flickered before him as a possibility. He was certainly unlikely to obtain it without the friendship of the King of France. It must have been difficult for a prelate who loved power so much to resist the chances of that great position.

The French King was at Saumur when he moved north with his company. He had with him an Italian ruling prince and the Mar-

---

[1] Cf. portrait reproduced facing p. 32.
[2] Cf. D. S. Chambers 'Cardinal Wolsey and the papal tiara', *Bulletin of the Institute of Historical Research*, xxxviii, no. 9.

3 Margaret, Marchioness of Dorset

The Lady Montegle.

4 Mary, Lady Monteagle

quis of Saluzzo, whose lands lay on his route to Italy. He proved to be among the most successful of the contestants in the tournaments. Beside the four French Cardinals there was also a papal nuncio and ambassadors from Venice, Mantua and Ferrara. There were also another independent ruler the Duke of Lorraine, and the royal Dukes of Bourbon, Alençon and Vendôme and the King of Navarre. There was a marcher Lord the Duke of Bouillon and those great names which would suggest the future, Guise, and La Trèmouille, Coligny,[1] Laval and Montmorency. The real point to remember is that these were all destined to go to Italy to fight. There was a sense in which the English lords and knights were civilians when compared to them.

It is not surprising that there were elements in the situation that were bound to rile King Francis. The King of England still used the title of King of France, which his ancestor Edward III had assumed before the outbreak of the Crecy war. Further his base was in the French town of Calais, which his ancestors had occupied. There was much play with the betrothal of King Henry's only daughter to the Dauphin, though both children were only four years of age.

Immediately the ceremonies were over King Henry retired to Calais, where he received a visit from the Emperor who came across from his town of Gravelines. As a result there came a different engagement, which Queen Catherine had always wanted, between the Princess Mary and the Emperor, although this had the disadvantage that he was some sixteen years her senior. In fact two years later England was at war with France in alliance with the Emperor; at the same time France did not suffer an invasion. Perhaps it cannot be said that the meeting at the Field of the Cloth of Gold was wholly useless. The promise that the two Kings had made to build a chapel dedicated to Our Lady of Friendship at their meeting place was naturally left unfulfilled.

[1] His son the future Amiral de Coligny was at this time a child a few months old at Châtillon-sur-Loing.

D

V

The Great Cardinal

The Cardinal looked after the King's policies, his works and pleasures. He had therefore his share in bringing about the promotion of Charles Brandon to be Duke of Suffolk. There is nothing enigmatic in his character and the dates of his high offices are known to us; there is little else. The date of his birth is unknown, but his father was killed at Bosworth by King Richard III, while holding the Earl of Richmond's standard. The boy was apparently brought up at the Court, but he is only heard of in the young King's reign, first as an esquire of the body, then as Sir Charles Brandon and in 1513 as Viscount Lisle.

The most detailed aspect of his life is the not very interesting question of his marriages. He received the Lisle peerage of Kingston Lisle in Berkshire as the result of his betrothal to Lady Lisle, a little girl who had become his ward on the death of her step-father Sir Thomas Knyvett. This betrothal was subsequently set aside and she died as the child bride of the Earl of Devon. Lord Lisle had made two earlier marriages. It appears that in the reign of Henry VII he had entered into a contract with Anne sister to Sir Anthony Browne, the celebrated courtier. He had then gone through a form of marriage with her aunt, the widowed Lady Margaret Mortimer, one of the orphan daughters of John Marquess of Montagu. Returning to Anne Browne,[1] he had had two daughters by her and then she died. Lady Margaret continued to plague him for many years. He finally obtained an annulment of

---

[1] Little is known of the Brandon family history, but he sought an application for the annulment of his marriage with Lady Margaret on the grounds that he and his wife were in the second and third degrees of affinity, that his wife and his first betrothed were within the prohibited degrees of consanguinity and that he was first cousin once removed of his wife's former husband.

this union, confirming the decision of the Consistory Court of London, from Pope Clement VII, then at Orvieto.

There is a certain mystery about his next adventure. There is said to have been a proposal that he should marry the Arch-duchess Margaret, Governess of the Low Countries and a daughter of the Emperor. But surely this could never have been considered by the House of Austria? At any rate he was created Duke of Suffolk and in 1516 married, instead, King Henry's sister Mary, the young widow of Louis XII. The King's attitude towards this marriage was ambivalent. But these marriages and his high offices gave us only the framework of Suffolk's life. He lived before the age of letter writing and left no enduring male posterity. The exact location of his estates and even the houses in which he lived are not known to us.[1]

He was tall and ruddy and a fit companion for all the young King's exercises. In later life, like his master, he became corpulent. It is clear that he was jealous of Wolsey. He lived through the religious changes and absorbed vast quantities of monastic land. There is no evidence that religion meant a thing to him. In dealing with the King he had one advantage; he was not a competitor in intelligence.

After the death of the King's sister the Queen of France, he married a fourth time, his young ward Catherine Willoughby, who had been destined for his dead son. He gradually faded out in his last years and died in 1543. The King had been accustomed all his life to his other Lords, to the Duke of Norfolk with his wolf-like countenance. It is likely that there was something appealing in a combination of stupidity just lit by cunning. Among all the great men of the high nobility Brandon was the only one whom the King had made. To use the old phrase of the Papal Court he alone was *ab eo creato*.

This was indeed a world in which the Cardinal and the King would rule together. All Wolsey's great powers were in fact a part of the apparatus of the English monarchy. In the first place he was Lord Chancellor. Then the many men who served him all gave glory to the kingdom; they were servants of the Cardinal of

---

[1] It should be said that he certainly lived for some time at Westhorpe near Bury St Edmunds.

England. It was indeed partly the King's youth, but still more the royal laziness, which had built up the Cardinal's position. In the first place the Cardinal was in London, which was so to speak the seat of Government, while the King was constantly travelling through the south counties. When he was young the King must have his fill of hunting. It seems that the Cardinal's main objective was to serve the King and that he really understood his sovereign. He grasped his need for the praise which came to him so easily. It was a Court which had but little trace of cynicism. There was no resemblance here to those lucid French courtiers who stood about the Valois King. In England men were simple and direct and full of praise. To use a homely phrase all men knew well the side on which their bread was buttered. The Cardinal also saw that it was well that no man should strive to thwart his sovereign's wishes. Cardinal Wolsey loved glory, but he was not covetous; there was no touch of meanness in his disposition.

He lived before the age of the great builders and he had, perhaps no more than his royal master a sense of what the palace might soon become. He was fond of the long galleries which he developed at Hampton Court and also built in his London mansion at York Place. He had an eye for the smaller detail, for example the external medallions which he placed at Hampton Court, a practice that he copied from those erected by the Cardinal d'Amboise at Gaillon, the country palace of the Archbishop of Rouen.

At the same time as soon as he noticed that the King's admiration for his works at Hampton Court was turning towards envy, he surrendered the place to him. This transaction took place in 1525. Certainly the King's failure to maintain his Spanish marriage was a misfortune for the Cardinal. It was not that Queen Catherine had ever liked him. He was too far removed from the severe Spanish Cardinals whom she had known at the Court of her parents the Castilian Kings. Still, friendly or unfriendly, she was an essentially stable factor and stability was what the Cardinal needed to maintain his rule.

His own personal preference had always favoured a French alliance. This was an understanding which English statesmen had pursued for the last three generations. No one in the immediate circle of the King of England was ever able to trust or understand the Emperor Charles. In these later years Wolsey was engaged upon the building up of the House of Christ Church. It was these operations, involving as they did the suppression of certain small religious houses permitted by the Holy See, which would give a foretaste of the destruction of the English monasteries. There was much that was old-fashioned in his mark of life. He could not foresee the way events were moving. His thought on politics and the state of nations was deep embedded in the fifteenth century.

VI

The Duke of Buckingham

In the first part of the reign the intention of the great landowners was to retain their large and varied properties and their local influence, intentions carried out in general with a certain negligence, and the purpose of the courtiers was for the most part to acquire some landed property. It was rare for either party to consider yet the building of a great house, and when this was done it bore no resemblance to the establishment of a great estate, a house with its gardens and surrounding parks, such as later became characteristic of the English countryside. It was not until the building of Longleat House, set in its wide park in the early part of the Elizabethan period, that this type of country palace was at last established.

The notion of defence against attack was slow in dying and certain elements inspired by these precautions are visible in almost all the larger houses which were built before the coming of the breach with Rome. The idea of defence was the negation of that desire for a tranquil privacy which would be one of the dominant characteristics in such a country palace as Hatfield would become in the succeeding century.

Further we know relatively little about the houses in which, for instance, the White Rose families lived. We can form no picture of the Marquess of Exeter's home at Horsley or even of his dower house at Columb John, and a portion of a five-storeyed slender tower before the entrance gate is all that remains of Warblington Castle, the Countess of Salisbury's residence.

The smaller type of building, the manor house, was still seen as embedded in its fields. The idea is expressed very clearly in Fitzherbert's *Book of Husbandrie* published in 1522. 'The manor house is sufficiently well builded with two cross chambers of stone, brick or timber with all manor houses of office within forth, two barns and an oxhouse, a hay house and a stable, a garden and an orchard.' A further element of impermanence was derived from the use of wood in such constructions.

In the first period of the reign two sections of the ruling class alone showed themselves as great builders, the old-established wealthy families and the abbots, who now sometimes constructed their own lodgings. In both cases there can be traced the gate-house *motif*. On the monastic side there is the singularly perfect example of Abbot Chard's tower and hall at Forde Abbey in Dorsetshire and the entrance gate to Montacute Priory in the adjacent county. From the more northern parts there is the heavier gatehouse at Saighton Grange in Cheshire. All these are stone.

There was a tendency to accept old-fashioned buildings, a rather surprising tendency of make-shift residence. Thus the Duke of Buckingham spent much of his time at Penshurst, where the still-surviving hall had dated from the fourteenth century. Some of the more recent castles were still in use like Bodiam and Hurstmon-ceux, the home of Lord Dacres of the South, among the water meadows in eastern Sussex. In many large houses of the period it is entrance gates or sometimes, as at Layer Marney, the entrance pile which now alone survives. Kirtling Tower in Cambridgeshire and Boarstall Tower near Thame are both striking examples, as is the gateway tower at Oxburgh. Naturally these are more often found in the brick counties.

In some parts of England the still constant use of wood explains the disappearance of certain houses. Some comments in John Leland's *Travels* bear on this point. 'So forth,' he wrote,[1] 'by Chiltern hills and woods to [Gaddesden?] where the Lord of Derby has a pretty manor place of timber. The old house of the Cheyneys is so translated by my Lord Russell that little or nothing of it re-maineth, and a great deal of the house is even newly set up made of brick and timber and fair lodgings are erected in the garden.' The buildings were put up about this time for Sir John Russell's marriage took place in the spring of 1526.

---

[1] *The Itinerary of John Leland in about 1535–1543*, ed. Lucy Toulmin Smith (1907), part I, pp. 164–5.

The first impression left by the great uncompleted palace of Thornbury is its immense extent. It reflects the rather lethargic mind of its creator, for the third Duke of Buckingham had been working on it for ten years before he met with his catastrophe. No architect seems to have been associated with this construction. It is high and grand and had it been completed it would have seemed unbalanced. This lack of proportion gives it a real ugliness. The four high bare towers with two smaller towers between them which were to form the western front would in effect have seemed top-heavy. The grey stone rose heavily, unbroken on the ground floor by any window spacing. On a ribbon over the main gateway there was sculptured an inscription: 'This gateway was begun in the yeare of our Lorde God 1511, the 2nd yeare of the reigne of Kynge Henry VIII, by me Edward, Duc of Buckingham, Earl of Hereford, Stafford and Northampton.'

Only one of the towers of the front, that at the southern corner, was ever completed and that has lost its crenellated parapet, although it retains its machicolation. This main front was to some extent still fortified. Gloucestershire in the recent wars had been a disturbed county. When completed this long western side would have been three hundred feet across. Inward from this there stretched two great ranges of building, the southern wing which was to contain a group of 'stately lodgings' in part completed and the northern side which held the great hall of the small old castle and a series of 'houses of office' opening out on to the kitchen court. There were great windows on the inner side containing long panes of glass in their stone settings. Some of the window-panes were curved with moulded glass. Above these rose the elaborate brick chimney stacks with all their varied heraldry. The main rooms would have looked on the privy garden, which opened out on to an orchard. There were flowers in beds and many roses. These great rooms were still unroofed; but with their lightness and the fresh air streaming in to them they would have been a vision of the future.[1]

Still, this link with the shape of things to come was accidental. The large windows were built on for glory and for ostentation.

---

[1] There is a detailed account of Thornbury Castle printed in H. Avray Tipping, *English Homes*, period II, vol. I, 1485–1558, pp. 79–82.

The normal situation at that time was one of small rooms, usually quite dark and enriched by tapestries and costly stuffs.

There is usually some problem about ancient buildings and at Thornbury the undecided question is where exactly the Duke lived when he visited his unfinished house. There was obviously some accommodation for at a later date King Henry and Anne Boleyn stayed there. But it is curious how little the King then knew about the private arrangements of an over-mighty subject.

It appears that Penshurst was the only one of the Duke's houses which the King visited. Five others were described as suitable for the King's occupation. There was Kimbolton Castle, 'a right goodly lodging', built within the previous sixty years by the first Duke's widow and now in great decay. There were also Stafford Castle and Maxstoke Castle, but the latter needed finishing plaster and new flooring and much glassing also was required.

Two smaller houses were noted as suitable for the royal purposes. One was the manor place of Bletchley, which was newly built with many lodgings and offices. The hall,[1] chapel, chamber, parlour and closets were ceiled with wainscot roofs, floors and walls, 'to the intent they may be used at pleasure without hangings'. The other was the manor of Writtle in Essex three miles from New Hall. This building had a stately stair, but as there was no hall a goodly and large parlour was used for this purpose. The moat was overgrown with wood and weeds, a spring ran through it. It was noted that at no great charge this could be made a convenient house for the King, 'when on occasion His Grace should be minded to remove from New Hall, and for hunting time in summer'.

The same description gives an account of the surroundings of Thornbury. It was stated that from the castle grounds posterns led out to the New Park, which contained about four miles within it and seven hundred deer. 'Nigh to the said New Park is another park called Marlewood, nothing between them but the breadth of a highway. It extends over three miles and contains three hundred deer. There is another park called Estewood within two miles of the said castle [of Thornbury] containing about seven miles with fallow deer and red deer also.' In building up these parks the Duke

---

[1] *Letters and Papers, Henry VIII*, vol. III, part I, 1519–23, p. 509.

had turned out many of his tenants. From these accounts we gain a certain impression of the Duke of Buckingham.

The Duke possessed the last of the great semi-feudal amalgams of landed property in the South of England. Since his father had rebelled against Richard III he had retained all his estates. Born in 1478 at Brecknock, which was the centre of what was almost his father's Welsh palatinate, he had inherited everything at the age of seven. He had been made a Knight of the Garter when he came of age. He was like some great mastodon, heavy, slow-moving with a tiny brain. But in any case he would not have been allowed to keep so much that seemed to trench upon the royal authority. What was needed to succeed at King Henry's early Court was to be gay and subservient and the Duke was neither.

It seems that he was always most impressed by the grandeur of his own descents. At the same time he was not in any special way the fruit of intermarriage. His mother was of an obscure stock the Woodvilles and her mother the Duchess of Bedford came from the great French house of Luxembourg de St Pol; in turn her mother was a Neapolitan. It was to the earlier generations that the *congeries* of intermarriage of the Staffords with the Nevilles, Beauchamps, Beauforts and Bohuns has belonged.

This was what determined the Stafford outlook. There is an arid note about all his arrangements. Until the very end the Duke was building up his marriages within this group, his two younger daughters married respectively the Earl of Westmorland and Lord Abergavenny, the heads of the two surviving branches of the House of Neville. His son the Earl of Stafford married Ursula, the Countess of Salisbury's eldest child. He himself had been affianced at the age of twelve to the fourth Earl of Northumberland's eldest daughter. She never seemed to have counted for very much in his affairs.

The history of his line was very blood-stained. His own father had been executed by Richard III and the Duke of Gloucester, through whom all his claims had come, by Richard II. His grandfather and great grandfather, the Earl of Stafford and the first Duke of Buckingham were both slain in the Wars of the Roses. He had inherited through many generations the office of Lord High Constable.

It appears that at the last the King was preoccupied by the castles that he held. Brecknock and Newport, which had a water gate that opened out upon the Bristol Channel, and, perhaps above all, Tonbridge. It was centuries since this last great appanage had been in the royal possession. It had come to the Staffords through the de Bohun heiress, who had married the Duke of Gloucester and the de Bohuns had had it as part of their share of the De Clare inheritance.

Stone in Staffordshire was still in some sense the burial place of the Duke's family, and there were all the many manors which had come down in the male line with the Earls of Stafford. There was part of the inheritance of the Earls of Albemarle, a series of lands in Holderness and a ferry service across the Humber. Away in the solitude of central Wales there stood Caurs Castle. On the other hand it seems there was no link with all the varied masses of the Stafford tenantry, they were too scattered. The whole estates are best conceived as a loosely held great area of landed property. There was nothing here which could resemble the power that the Percies were able to exercise upon the gentry and the yeomen and the tenants in the North. The Duke was ungenial and too much bound up with his own small class, the old high fifteenth-century families, who were now failing. This is, perhaps, a sufficient background to explain the Duke's disaster.

From one angle it cannot be said that the Duke of Buckingham's fall was unexpected. He was a lack-lustre uninteresting chief, but all the same he was still the head of a great and out-moded organization. It was a pity that there was no way of removing him, except by death. The practice of exiling fallen politicians to foreign countries did not begin until the later centuries.

It is curious that Cardinal Wolsey, although the chief object of his animus, was opposed to his prosecution. Perhaps, in a vague way he foresaw the consequences that his execution would entail. It was the King himself who proved so adamant. Supposing that the charges against the Duke were true, it is still hard to see how he could come to be involved in them. Even if the King should die without sons it is difficult to see how the Crown could come to him. The Duke's old-fashioned thought probably excluded the idea of a female sovereign. If that be admitted, it is true that in the early days of the reign some sort of hazardous claim might be put forward once the King was dead. This would mean that the King's own sisters and when she was born, in 1516, the King's daughter would be excluded as well as the Countess of Devon and the Countess of Salisbury. One has to assume that he neglected the claim of the last of the de la Poles, perhaps on some line which excluded the whole House of York: this involves a large assumption.

One accusation appears quite pointless, the assertion that the Duke is said to have made to Lord Abergavenny as they paced together in his gallery at Blechingly that he had a document which proved that Edmund Beaufort Duke of Somerset was legitimate.[1] The other accusation refers to the alleged statement of a 'holy Carthusian', Dom Nicholas Hopkins, the vicar of the Charterhouse of Hinton in Somerset, that King Henry would have no sons and that the Crown would pass to him. The Duke was betrayed by members of his council, by Robert Gilbert his chancellor and John Delacourt his chaplain. It appears that they felt that this was the only way to save their lives, being servants of so rash and garrulous a master.

The Duke was at Thornbury when he was ordered to come to London in 1521. He rode up slowly through the April weather and on arrival at the manor of the Rose was conveyed to the Tower. He was tried and executed one month later. There was about this trial that note of corporate responsibility which characterized all the great events of the King's reign which might give rise to controversy. King Henry's policy and his position had no resemblance to that of the tyrants in fifteenth-century Italy. It may perhaps be best described as an oligarchy under the royal guidance. The actual charge against the Duke of Buckingham, that of imagining the death of his sovereign, could not easily be denied and, if proved, could have only one outcome. Weight was given to a statement made by the Duke some eight years previously and vouched for by his chancellor to the effect that the Earl of Warwick (the only son of the Duke of Clarence) had been put to death and that God

[1] The Duke's grandmother was a co-heiress and not the sole heiress of this Duke; but in any case Margaret Countess of Richmond was the heiress of Duke John, his elder brother.

would punish this by not suffering the King's issue to prosper as appeared by the death of his son.

The court before whom he was brought was composed of a cross-section of the peerage. Under the presidency of the Duke of Norfolk there sat the Duke of Suffolk, the Marquess of Dorset, the Earls of Derby, Devon, Kent, Shrewsbury and Worcester, the Prior of St John's, and Lords Cobham, Dacre of the South, Delawarr, Ferrers, Fitzwarine, Mountjoy and Roos. No North country peer had been invited.[1] Among other absentees the Earl of Arundel was a very old man and the Earl of Oxford a very young one, still on account of his extravagance in the Duke of Norfolk's care. Norfolk and the Duke of Suffolk were the only two among those present who could be described as within the Duke of Buckingham's restricted circle. The Earl of Devon, who later became Marquess of Exeter, was the solitary peer present who was himself the head of a 'White Rose' stock. There were a number of other absentees mainly among the less important barons; but it seems nevertheless to have been a characteristic representation of the House of Lords chosen to carry through an important measure.

The circumstances of the attack upon the Duke were responsible for two other elements among the surviving documentation; a fairly complete analysis of the Duke's debts and what is more interesting a note of the shrines and religious houses with which he was in contact. He received considerable loans from the Abbot of Westminster and the Bishop of Durham and lands were alienated to the Duke of Suffolk, Sir William Compton, Sir Richard Sacheverell and Thomas Kytson, merchant. Kytson who reappears later in the reign as the builder of Hengrave Hall, was probably a money lender.

In his sedate way the Duke appears to have been something of a gambler. There are notes of his loss at dice to Lord Fitzwalter and also to Lord Burgoyne (clearly a mistake for Burgavenny or Abergavenny) and Lord Montagu. After the record of some smaller sums there is a note of a loss 'at dice to my Lord Montagu, £65 2s 9d'. Then comes a further list of the Duke's indebtedness. 'Lost at shooting £31 6s 8d. Lost to the King at tennis £64. Lost at

---

[1] These included the Earls of Northumberland and Westmorland and Lords Clifford, Dacre of the North, Darcy, Latimer and Scrope of Bolton.

dice in my new place with the Duke of Suffolk and the French
Queen £76 1s 6d.' Similar expenses were incurred upon his
journeys between Thornbury and London. 'Lost at Sir Maurice
Berkeley's £6 13s 4d lost to my brother Wiltshire and to Lord
Montagu £40.' On the other hand there is a note made about this
time. 'Put in a bag £43 6s 5d won at dice.'

There are also a variety of charges. These begin with the ordinary expenses of a rich man living in the country. His gifts to
gypsies, 'To certain Egyptians at Thornbury, 40s.' He gave 13s 4d
for a throstle bird, and paid Francis Aderley a shilling for a jer-
faucon, which he took up in the fields at Tortworth. There were
sums to the gatekeeper at Gloucester as he rode into that town.

There was a gift to the servants of the Abbot of Gloucester for
showing him three great horses at Llanthony, and then we come
to all his expenses of a religious character. These were sometimes
gifts made on his accustomed way to London by Cirencester or
Malmesbury, an oblation to the relic of the Holy Blood at Hailes
and a note on the visit of his brother-in-law the Earl of Northumberland to this same shrine. There were oblations to the shrines of
Our Lady at Kingswood, St Aldhelm at Malmesbury, to the
shrine of the Child of Grace at Reading and to Our Lady of Eton.
There were also offerings in Somerset, to Our Lady of Belhouse at
Bristol, sums payable to the Abbot of St Augustine's in that city,
and gifts at Glastonbury in honour of St Joseph of Arimathea.
Further afield there was an offering sent to the Shrine of Our Lady
of Walsingham. There were sums paid by his chaplain to Brian
Tuke for four pieces of Arras and expenses for the dean of the
Duke's chapel. There was a petition to the Pope's collector for a
dispensation on the grounds of consanguinity to enable Lord
Abergavenny to marry his daughter Lady Mary.

Two entries have a more domestic touch. One is an offering to
John Glade, a hermit formerly the Duke's servant and the other is
a note of the expenses of his servant Francis when he went to the
abbey of St Albans to pray for a cure that would heal his head and
neck. These entries tend to show an intimacy with the religious
shrines and houses which by the sixteenth century had become
perhaps politically undesirable. One of the last payments of the
Duke was a sum to his gardener at Thornbury Castle for laying

out his heraldic emblem, the Stafford knots, among the flower beds in the privy garden.

A certain care was taken in the breaking up of the Duke's great estates. An annuity was reserved to the Duchess of Buckingham and was paid to her until she died some nine years later. The lands round Stafford Castle were given back in time to her son Lord Stafford. As for Thornbury the castle remained unfinished, but was used as a quasi-royal residence. It was visited later once by Henry VIII accompanied by Anne Boleyn in her short reign. Kimbolton Castle likewise remained in the King's possession. It was here that Catherine of Aragon resided during her last months, and here she died.

Two gifts were made to the men who had been ordered to bring the Duke to London. Sir William Compton received the castle and park of Maxstoke besides other manors and Sir Richard Weston received the site on which he was to build the great house of Sutton Place. This last grant was made on the day of the Duke's execution. The estates in Essex were allocated in large holdings; six manors went to the Earl of Essex and almost as many to Sir Henry Marney.[1] The latter also secured the Duke's rights in the borough of Buckingham.

Most of the land went to courtiers or to great peers, who had close Court connections. These last included the Marquess of Dorset and two other members of the Grey family, the Earl of Worcester, who received a single Kentish manor and the Earl of Devon, who received some land in Cornwall. It is surprising to find Lord Devon as the head of a 'White Rose' family, but he was at this time still close to the King and it was probably part of his new office as High Steward of the Duchy. The honour of Holderness in Yorkshire was granted to the Earl of Northumberland and the remaining manors there came in 1527 to this eldest son. The stewardships of the Duke's lordships in Wales went to Lord Ferrers.

Two very different families date their rise from their possession of the Duke's estates. Penshurst appears to have remained among

---

[1] There were other considerable blocks. Four manors in Wiltshire went to Sir Edward Darell and six in Norfolk, including Welles, Blakeney and Sheringham, to John Rushbrook, yeoman of the Crown, thus setting up this family in East Anglia, Grants in March 1522, *Letters and Papers*.

the royal lands until it was granted in 1552 to Sir Henry Sidney, whose descendants made it famous. Writtle also passed to the Crown and later became the fulcrum of Sir William Petre's properties.

At the same time there were many courtiers who received one manor each. Lord Essex received Bedminster in Somerset and Sir John Raglan Pentkelly *Angliae* in Glamorgan. The names one comes across are most familiar and they include Sir Thomas Boleyn, Sir Nicholas Carew, Lord Richard Grey, Sir Richard Jerningham, Sir William Skevington, Sir Edward Neville, Sir Richard Guldeford and Sir Gilbert Tailboys. John Scott gained the Lordships of Camberwell and Peckham. Sir Thomas More received the manor of South in Kent in the year in which he received his knighthood. These were not 'new men'; they were on the other hand a normal list of courtiers most in view.

Among the most characteristic of the beneficiaries was Sir William Sandys. He was Knight of the Garter and Treasurer of Calais. He received two of Buckingham's manors including Stratton St Margaret. He also became keeper of the forest of Alice Holt in Hampshire, where masts were already prepared for the Royal Navy. He held a wood court in the forest every sixth week. Besides this, there was a reversionary interest in the manor of Wardelham after the rights of the Earl of Arundel and Lord Maltravers.

Sandys was to be the builder of the Vyne.

5 Archbishop Warham

6 Bishop Fisher

VII

The Courtiers' Homes

Among the courtiers' houses which date from the first part of King Henry's reign the Vyne is perhaps the best example that survives to us. It was within range of the movement of the Court as then conceived, standing just twelve miles from the King's hunting lodge at Easthampstead, which was within the policies of Windsor Castle. It lay northwards from Basingstoke and therefore close to one of the main roads which the Lords from the West Country would use on their approach to Court and capital.

Set on those low chalk downs around the head waters of the Loddon, it was not precisely on the site of any predecessor. It was not a house that was conceived to be in any way defensible. Sir William Sandys would use the brick which was only then beginning to be baked in Hampshire. He had been born about 1470 and therefore belonged to the eldest generation among King Henry's courtiers. He was shrewd and made use of his popularity. A letter from Bishop Fox of Winchester to the Cardinal brings out this point. He is speaking of a riot at Southampton in the early summer of 1517. 'No-man,' wrote the Bishop,[1] 'could have been more fit to order the matter than Sandys, who is among them mayor, bailiff and entire ruler of the town. With his authority from the King and the love he has among the people he can do more than the mayor and all the officers of the town and port.' He made his way smoothly in the days of Cardinal Wolsey's power; but he was too well-born really to like him.

Sir William had married while quite young a wealthy heiress Margery the niece of Sir Reginald Bray of Eaton Bray in Bedfordshire. He had been an early supporter and something of a favourite

[1] *Letters and Papers, Henry VIII*, Addenda, vol. I, part I. Letter dated 10 May 1517.

E

of the Earl of Richmond before he reached the English Crown. He obtained Lord Audley's properties after his attainder; but his real interest derives from his interest and skill in architecture. Bray is supposed to have been responsible for the design of St George's Chapel at Windsor Castle, where he was buried. It seems possible, for there is no direct evidence, that he may have had some share in the building of the Vyne.

The house retains the gallery and the chapel and the chapel parlour that Sandys erected. In this the Vyne resembled the accommodation that Richard Sackville was building at Buckhurst at this period. The King visited Sandys for two nights in 1516; the chapel parlour has linenfold panelling dating from this time.

In 1523 he was raised to the peerage as Lord Sandys of the Vyne and three years later he received the great post of Lord Chamberlain. He was always a somewhat isolated figure, very consciously the founder of a dynasty which did not in fact survive. He was involved in none of the skeins of relationship. His sister made two marriages of influence, first with Lord Neville and then with Lord Darcy, but both away in the North Country.

He was one of the King's favourite hunting companions; he was keeper for life of Easthampstead, the nearest royal park. As his private chapel shows he was deeply attached to all the old-world ceremonies. He was also like most rather simple men, who rose solely through the Court, a devoted and unquestioning Royalist. It can be seen from his correspondence that Sandys was an open character and he thus appealed to that love of unfettered open contact which was one side of the King's nature, when he was young.

The Duke of Buckingham could look down on the monasteries with good-natured patronage; but men of Sandys' class were never easy with the monks as landlords. In the changes that lay ahead one temptation alone was irresistible, the opportunity to gain monastic land.

There was something soldierly about Lord Sandys' house. This is clear as we read through the inventories made at his death. He belonged to the times before the world was lavish. There were of course the royal beds that he had bought, the King's of green velvet with cloth of gold. But the gallery was very empty; it contained only two small tables, a cupboard of wainscot and a Spanish folding chair. The rooms were all hung with tapestry, although it might be only with hangings of 'imagery sore worne'. There were fifty-two rooms in the house, but they contained only nineteen chairs covered with Flanders work. The rest were seats and long movable benches.

The next three houses to be considered were not, like the Vyne, in the immediate neighbourhood of the Court and it seems likely that courtiers would have some temporary accommodation in or near Greenwich or Windsor. Within half a century the new frequency of dated and addressed personal correspondence would enable us to plot exactly what in the early part of Henry's reign must be surmise.

Another of the Henrican country houses is Compton Wynyates, the most beautiful of them all, as it stands in its narrow combe on the north-western Cotswold slopes looking down into Warwickshire. Although in a stone country, it is a mass of old red brick, now pale with age. There is an effect of silvery brown against the worn stone slates. But it somehow does not give the effect of a house of King Henry's day. It was worked over in succeeding generations and the effect is contrived and Elizabethan.

The family too, which created it is likewise Elizabethan and later Cavalier in its main emphasis for Sir William Compton, another of King Henry's earlier courtiers, was cut off in 1528 by the sweating sickness. He was a man of an old-fashioned piety which will be described in detail in the chapter on the English priesthood. He was a great accumulator of offices and of estates. The former were all scattered, but the land was held together under the guardianship of the Earls of Shrewsbury. The fourth Earl married his daughter Lady Anne Talbot to the young heir Peter Compton, who passed his whole life in his minority. He was born in 1522, married at nineteen, had a son and died aged twenty. The properties then passed into another twenty years of tutelage. For this reason the wide estates of the family, which would later receive the earldom and marquessate of Northampton, remained in chrysalis.

Similarly linked with the Duke of Buckingham is Hengrave Hall on the flat lands in Suffolk to the north of Bury St Edmunds. Sir Thomas Kytson who bought the manor from the Duke in 1527, was, like Sir William Compton, one of his creditors. He was the only example among these men of a new mercantile fortune, a Londoner of influence trading with Antwerp. The interesting factor about the house is that we can tell in this case where the materials came from. Hengrave Hall was rather later in date than the two others; it was building between 1530 and 1538. The brick used came for the most part from the brick fields of the abbey of Bury St Edmunds. In 1530 124,000 were purchased from the abbot. It seems that the stone was brought from the King's Cliff quarries in Northamptonshire and was transported by waterway to Brandon or Wordlington in Suffolk and thence by cart. The oak timber came largely from Combey Wood. The new house occupied the site and also used the materials of the old manor built in the fourteenth century by Sir Thomas de Hengrave. There were summer and winter parlours and both a candle chamber and a candle house, one for storing and the other for manufacturing candles. The tapestries were all obtained through Sir Thomas's own business contacts with Flanders.

These are the interesting details about the house, which is itself somewhat amorphous. Sir Thomas Kytson died in 1541. He was one of those who benefited from the Court's policies rather than himself a courtier. His wealthy widow married the Earl of Bath, whom she brought to this new house.

East Barsham Manor is a much more remarkable early Tudor house lying in an isolated part of Norfolk, stranded and nearly complete. It appears to have been built by an almost unknown Sir Henry Fermor, who did not belong to the Easton Neston family. Built of coloured brick between 1520 and 1530 it stands some six miles inland from Wells-next-the-Sea. It has the gatehouse arch, which was characteristic of the earlier time, and many pinnacles. There are ten shafted chimney stacks with moulded curved sections of terra cotta, enriched with roses, diapers and fleur-de-lys.

VIII

The House of Howard

It was May 1525 and the first weeks of the East Anglian summer had come to where the big ancient castle of Framlingham lay stranded in the level fields. It was far from any real centre on the southern edge of the former Mowbray inheritance. Eastward the flat lands stretched towards Saxmundham and the sea. There was nothing changed in that high keep from the middle years of the fifteenth century and the old Duke of Norfolk lay dying there.

It is at this stage that the House of Howard emerges as a set of persons into the stream of English life. The first and second Dukes of Norfolk of that line are alike indecypherable. They lived before the age of portraiture; there are few letters. All that we can now see is that they possessed the gift of acquisition and a large share of tenacity. They appear to have been earnest in support of Edward IV and of King Richard. It was from the latter that they gained the Norfolk dukedom. This had not unnaturally been lost at Bosworth and the old Duke had laboured all his life to re-acquire it. He had been guardian of the North for many years and had won the fight at Flodden when he was seventy.

It seems that he though not his son, appealed to Queen Catherine; perhaps she saw a resemblance to the warrior Dukes of Alba and to Gonzalo de Cordova. Lord Herbert of Cherbury's stories of Norfolk's opposition to the young Cardinal make little sense to us. The King in his first years gave great rewards to those to whom he was at heart indifferent. It was part of the Castilian atmosphere of the reign's beginning. Suddenly in 1525 the House of Howard comes out into the light of day. And it is worth attempting to give

as complete a picture as we can of the Duke of Norfolk and his
situation for he was to remain a crucial figure in Court and Government throughout the reign.

The new Duke, whose portrait[1] now at Windsor Castle is one of
Holbein's masterpieces, was at that time fifty-two years of age. The
Venetian Ambassador has described him as 'small and spare in
person, his hair black'. He had skin the colour of dark parchment,
thin lips, a long high-bridged nose, eyes not piercing, but very
cold. His health was delicate. In middle life he had become rheu-
matic; his digestion was in time impaired.

He had received many wardships. He was the friend, the well-
paid friend to many who were in the class below his own. He had a
knowledge of the trading conditions in East Anglia, a satisfaction
in hunting suitable to his position and apparently no more interest
in letters than a nobleman would require, although he spoke
French with some elegance. His financial sense was keen and he
had a feeling for jewels of real value. Ceremonial appealed to him
and the splendour of every-day costume, the Burgundian guards
of black velvet on a gown of tawny velvet-silk, which the age in-
dulged. He was pliant with a quick practical mind and a keen
scent for danger. The acquisition of property, especially landed
property, was pursued with a relentless satisfaction. Great offices
had already come to him. He had received the earldom of Surrey,
which had belonged to the Mowbrays and the Warennes, ten
years before as well as the post of Lord High Admiral. His father
had resigned to him his post as Lord Treasurer of England two
years previously.

The Duke suffered from matrimonial troubles. His first wife had
been high-born and consumptive, their children sickly. The Lady
Anne had been one of the daughters of Edward IV and the sister
of Queen Elizabeth, who had married Henry VII. After his first
wife died, her children having pre-deceased her, Surrey had
married Lady Elisabeth Stafford, the fourteen-year-old daughter
of the Duke of Buckingham. She was a termagant and twenty-
three years his junior. Their married life broke up the year after
he inherited the dukedom. Living in her dower house at Red-
bourne, she remained a burden to him. At Kenninghall he kept

[1] Reproduced facing p. 96.

his mistress Elizabeth Holland, sister to his steward and some relative to Lord Hussey, that ill-omened name.

He was always at ease with those below him like the East Anglian gentry from whom he sprang; the Pilgrims of Grace would listen to him. His mother and his stepmother both belonged to the same grouping, his mother the heiress of the Tilneys of Ashwell Thorpe and her successor, a cousin of that same stock. His stepmother the Duchess Agnes, now aged forty-seven, retired to the large rather disordered manor house at Horsham St Faith to the north of Norwich with her six children. His two sons, who would come into his life, were still both growing. He was the only adult male of his own house; he had to construct his power without assistance.

Like all those who had built up their own estates, he looked with a cold eye upon monastic properties. Monks' estates were in his judgement too large within the eastern counties. As far as religion is concerned, his attitude is often misconstrued. It seems that he was in general a Conservative and that he liked the appurtenances of his great position, the religious ceremonial is an example. But then he could not approach the sacraments, his private life prevented that and to the very core he was a Regalian. He would follow where the King might lead him.

He was solitary as those who would prosper in that reign were bound to be. He provided his young stepsisters with great marriages,[1] except for Lady Catherine who married Sir Rhys ap Griffith, the heir of a high Welsh family. But he took no man for his ally except for his political arrangement with Bishop Gardiner.

In his course he had two dangers. His family were more Catholic than he was and this applied especially to Duchess Agnes. And then finally his young heir grew to manhood and in time destroyed him, almost accidentally. In the later years of the Cardinal's power there was no great lord who was so ready to serve his sovereign as the Duke of Norfolk.

Framlingham still remains, but Kenninghall, his much more modern palace, has disappeared. It lay in isolated country to the north of the upper reaches of the Waveney and a few miles to the west of where the railway line now runs from Ipswich to Norwich past Tivetshall St Margaret. He had pulled down the old manorial

[1] They were given in marriage to the Earls of Oxford, Derby and Sussex.

hall and had built up a house in two main courts with chequered brickwork. We have an account of the house as it was some ten years later.[1] This may have some resemblance to Cardinal Wolsey's portions of Hampton Court. The Duke's own rooms were in the second court above the chapel. They were furnished with hangings of 'Imagen'. A crimson and white canopy stood over the great bed. Strips of Turkey carpet, not to be found in the King's palaces, covered the floor. There were also chairs covered with Bruges satin with white and yellow cushions.

There were six chaplains and in the oak presses forty copes.[2] Over the high altar there was a picture upon wainscoting of Christ's birth, passion and resurrection.

These details provide an example of our difficulty in attempting to rebuild the life of the English leaders in the sixteenth century. The light beats only on the Court.

We can, however, examine the domestic surroundings of one of the Duke of Norfolk's friends, who left him the guardian of his co-heiresses and of their property, that great uncompleted house which has always been known as Layer Marney Towers. It stands in Essex and its battlements look south across the fields towards the estuary of the Blackwater. It lay beyond the immediate Norfolk influence and rather within the sphere of the old Earl of Sussex, a veteran connected with the Duke by various titles.[3] The Radcliffes were a great family of the second rank; extravagant; not lasting. They were conservative and pliant, but mainly pliant. They are now forgotten for they had no leaders. The Sussex influence must be mentioned here for it had its effect in the disposal of the two co-heiresses. These were little girls aged ten and eight, when they fell into the Duke of Norfolk's custody. The property was consider-able but recently acquired, a string of manors brought together in the official life of the first Lord Marney, the grandfather of the little girls. It also included the Newburgh inheritance in East Dorset, which had belonged to the girls' mother.

[1] Cf. Neville Williams, *Thomas Howard 4th Duke of Norfolk* (1964).
[2] *Norfolk Archaeology*, vol. VII, pp. 284–5.
[3] The headquarters of this family was at New Hall, the old palace of Beaulieu, which Henry VIII no longer wanted. The first Earl of Sussex had married Lady Elizabeth Stafford, the Duchess of Norfolk's aunt and his heir Lord Fitzwalter had married Lady Elizabeth Howard, the Duke's young step-sister.

The arrangements made were normal for their class and period. The elder daughter was betrothed in succession to two of the Earl of Sussex's younger sons and the younger daughter married. Lord Thomas Howard, later first Viscount Howard of Bindon in Dorset, the Duke's own younger boy. The survival of the house is unusual.

The principal remains are essentially a gatehouse with four towers built in the brickwork of the eastern counties. This was to open out into an inner court. The two main towers were each eight storeys high. Part of the west wing beyond the towers had been completed. Some of the decoration was elaborate and it is clear that Italian terra-cotta workers were employed. It was after all quite close to London. In certain ways the detail lacks sophistication. One gains the impression that no architect was ever concerned with Layer Marney. Probably the work went up in the last years of the first Lord Marney, who died in 1523, and then was carried forward in a hurried fashion by his only son. Perhaps the second and last Lord Marney, who died in 1525, may have been tubercular; the architectural details have something feverish.

There are various reasons for this strange survival. The family had long been settled there, but the house was in no sense the centre of a laid-out estate. The first Lord Marney was a lucky courtier who had acquired some manors at the break-up of the Duke of Buckingham's great properties. Had the Marneys gone forward to their earldom the Towers would have long ago been taken down; but there was no one to carry forward the family aggregate. The courtier Sir Bryan Tuke, a relative and dependent of the Howards, took over the house on a short tenancy. But no mansion house was ever built there and there was therefore no reason to destroy this strange beginning. As far as the Duke of Norfolk was concerned, his interest was concentrated on the Dorset manors of the younger Marney heiress, which formed an appanage for his second son.

Norfolk's real concerns were nation-wide. Just before his father's death he was involved with Lord Monteagle's inheritance in the North of England. This old peer, the first of his line, was a younger son of the first Earl of Derby and had commanded one of the wings at Flodden under the Duke's father. The details of the arrangements at his death throw a vivid light on the contacts of the North Country peers in the years before the monasteries had been destroyed. They show one of the larger houses in the English countryside before the Reformation broke upon them.

Lord Monteagle had inherited Hornby Castle from his childless wife, who was the heiress of the North Country branch of the Haringtons. It was a remote property on the low ground of the Lune valley where that river flows southward from Kirkby Lonsdale below the northern bastions of the Bowland Forest. It is changed now and tame. There is nothing to remind us of the Monteagles, which in any case was a confected title[1] and not a place name. The village is dominated by the frowning castle constructed by the Georgian Dukes of Leeds and contains the priest's house, a Jane Austen building, in which Dr Lingard wrote his *History of England*.

Lord Monteagle was at this time isolated, confined to his chamber by old age and the gout. He was again a widower and the head of his house the Earl of Derby was a young boy. His own only son was fifteen years of age. His financial affairs were in some disorder. Cardinal Wolsey himself was well aware that there was much jewellery about the house. Shortly before his death, Monteagle asked his friends Lord Darcy and Sir John, later Lord Hussey, to come and visit him. This meant considerable journeys for Darcy lived at Templehurst, north of Doncaster in the East Riding, and Hussey even further away, at Sleaford in Lincolnshire. Darcy was a fellow-soldier and almost his contemporary; they were both Knights of the Garter. Darcy was rather more pious than that age required. He had been supported by Queen Catherine; he belonged to the Castilian period of King Henry's reign.

Lord Monteagle died leaving his son's marriage to Lord Darcy and his guardianship between Darcy and Hussey. At this point the Duke of Norfolk intervened[2] offering to marry the young Monteagle to his daughter and to prevent the executors from embezzling his goods. The boy himself applied to the King for permission to arrange his own marriage. In this matter Norfolk was unsuccessful

---

[1] This title was formed by the King's own thoughtfulness out of the Mount on which he had fought at Flodden and the Eagle of the Stanley crest.

[2] Cf. a letter to Cardinal Wolsey dated 15 April 1523.

and in time the boy married Lady Mary Brandon,[1] the Duke of Suffolk's eldest child. An inventory drawn up at this occasion shows what Lord Monteagle had in his possession.

In the first place it should be made quite clear that an undefined number of leaves are missing from this inventory.[2] The glimpse it gives is partial, but not without interest. Thus in regard to livestock the only reference is to Lord Monteagle's 115 wethers on his sheep run up on Bowland. Again there is no reference to arms or armour and the only mention of his clothes is a full description of his Garter robes, 'a blue velvet mantle with a Garter on the left shoulder, lined with white sarcenet for the chapel at Windsor. Scarlet hose with guarded black velvet about the thighs.'

On the other hand the account of the contents of his wine cellar appears complete, although the quantities are not described. 'Red wine, claret wine, white wine.' There is a note 'Old claret for vinegar' and a reference to Malmesey and Muscadel. It seems likely that the wine had been brought from abroad to that great natural harbour which washes the entrance gates to Furness Abbey and from thence along the shores of Morecambe Bay and by the rough lanes of the low country between Carnforth and Hornby.

Another aspect of Monteagle's goods which seems complete is the list of the assorted jewellery. This included 'a broken gold chain of forty-eight links of Paris work; two emeralds set in gold; a white sapphire. A pomander with stones and pearls. A gold double rose. Two gold buttons, blue enamelled. Three strings of pearls containing 141. A gold chain with a George that my Lord wore daily.' There are here two interesting comments. 'A fork for green ginger' and 'a small gold ball for warming my Lord's drink'. Some details are given of his silver. 'Six bowls of silver, parcel gilt; a shaving basin of silver, parcel gilt. Two square salts with an eagle on the cover. A standing cup with a cover, graven with flowers and a portcullis. Six apostle spoons.'

There was also a covering for a horse litter of green sarcenet guarded with red tinsel satin. A grey gelding was given to Sir John Hussey and two horses for the horse litter to Lord Darcy.

---

[1] Cf. Holbein's drawing of Mary Lady Monteagle reproduced facing p. 49.
[2] *Letters and Papers, Henry VIII*, 1521–3, pp. 1253–7.

This seems to explain how that ancient man could move for distances about the countryside.

A note set out details of the financial position. There were debts owed by Lord Monteagle to the Abbots of Furness and Vale Royal and to Sir Robert Tempest. 'My Lord's debts to the King' were set down at £111. In the inventory at Hornby £800 was noted and there was £366 at Whalley. Presumably this referred to the monastery there. The financial dealings between the abbots on the one hand and the rural peers and greater squires upon the other is an aspect of North Country Catholicism that has not yet been examined.

The furniture of the house at Hornby is hardly mentioned. There is a reference to feather beds in the nursery. What is given in great detail is the chapel stuffs and furniture. In the chapel at Hornby Castle there were two altar cloths of 'awresse'. It is suggested that this means 'arras' and this would be possible if it was really an altar covering that was in view. There were two fine tapestry hangings on the walls. In the closet chapel there was a table of the Salutation of Our Lady, all gilt, and two trunks and three baskets full of old writing. In the chamber next the wardrobe there were hangings of 'versours' and green say, lined with canvas. In the nursery there were two images, one of Jesus and the other of St John's head. There was an assortment in the gilt chamber. An altar cloth. An image of Our Lady and St Anne, all gilt. A little book called *The Chronicles*. A printed book called *Bartilmeus de Proprietatione Rerum*. A holy water stock of latten.

In these notes one can trace the lineaments of an old-fashioned house in which the Roman Mass was still important. Priests must have played their part in such a *ménage*, although there is no explicit reference to them. Lord Darcy and Lord Hussey both made forward. In the old-fashioned sense they were busy men; they both went down in the catastrophe of the Pilgrimage of Grace. If the wide English scene is now considered, the Church of Rome has entered on her Indian summer.

IX

The English Priesthood

In the last years before the Reformation the body of the clergy in England were divided into two sections which could be defined quite clearly; those who were in some ways involved in the administration and the rest of the ordinary parochial priesthood. This was a situation which was found reflected through most of the different countries in Western Europe. The smaller body can be recognized quite easily. It included all those prelates whose lives were given up to or involved with the service of the State, sometimes as ambassadors, sometimes as civil servants or administrators. It may be said to have included the whole body of bishops and the holders of deaneries. They all had some importance to the Government for the bishops had seats in the House of Lords.

The much larger body had no such pretensions. They were either assistant priests or chaplains or the holders of benefices, sometimes of more than one. The archdeaconries were in general the highest offices to which they could attain. Their secretarial work, when this was undertaken, was for the peers or for the gentry, not for the Crown. They were quite outside the *cursus honorum*. In addition to their parochial duties, they acted as both secretaries and agents. It is difficult to discover much about them. We can make certain casts to build up information.

The testamentary dispositions can show us how the more modern type of chantry was built up, an example is the will[1] of Sir William Compton, the builder of Compton Wynyates. This was signed in 1522 and the first Lord Marney had been named as the executor. Sir William was at that time forty and had been a ward of Henry VII and something of a favourite in the earlier portions of the

[1] Cf. *Letters and Papers of Henry VIII*, 1526–8, pp. 1942–3.

reign. He was a very wealthy man, whose offices will be mentioned when he died eventually in 1528. He had proposed to marry the Countess of Salisbury when she became a widow in 1519. He married late in life, having lived for a period in adultery with Lady Hastings, whose husband later became the first Earl of Huntingdon and who was herself the daughter of the second Duke of Buckingham. He had thus placed himself in the centre of the old-fashioned world.

By his will he left forty pairs of vestments to be distributed among the parishes of Warwickshire and Worcestershire situated nearest to his property. He also bequeathed to the abbey of Winchcomb his wedding gown of satin to make a vestment that the monks might pray for the souls of his ancestors. He willed that a tomb of alabaster should be prepared for his father beside his own grave. Two chantries were to be founded at his manor of Compton, where daily services were to be held for the King and the Queen, my Lady Anne Hastings, his wife and ancestors and for himself. The priests were to be appointed by the Abbot of Winchcomb or should he fail to do this by the Abbot of Evesham. The chapel was to be constructed in his house at Compton Wynyates.

In almost the same year there is an account[1] of the contents of the private chapel of the Marquess of Exeter. These details serve to build up the picture of the chaplains' life. There were kept in the press a pair of vestments of blue velvet, three *ditto* of black velvet, and one each of green velvet and of white and crane-coloured damask. There were two matins books of 'my Lady's Grace', one covered with tawny velvet with silver and gilt clasps, the other with black velvet with silver and gilt clasps engraved. Among the books in the chapel were copies of *Ortus vocabulorum*, *Catholica* and *Legenda aurea*, and also a book of law.

From these accounts one obtains an impression of the priests who lived quietly in these backwaters. In the second case they may have perhaps gone forward in due time to such advowsons as Lord Exeter had in his gift. One is reminded of the situation which existed until the break-up of the Hapsburg Empire in the archdiocese of Esztergom. There certain magnates kept some priests

---

[1] An account of the Marquess of Exeter's household dated 2 January 1525, *Letters and Papers of Henry VIII*, 1523–5, p. 1677.

throughout their lives on their properties, moving first as curates and then as rectors among the four or five contiguous parishes which served the wide estates in the plain of Hungary.

Another aspect of the life of the priesthood is revealed by the contemporary memoranda, when these are sufficiently complete. The best surviving example from this period is an account of the possessions of Thomas Dalby, who was in 1526 stationed at York and later became Archdeacon of Richmond.

It represents an ordinary secular priest of the most prosperous type. It should be read with a certain care. The constantly re-iterated note of 'say' hangings represents a rather coarse and heavy stuff, certainly relatively inexpensive. It suggests a condition of prosperity, but not of luxury. The account begins with a list of Dalby's possessions in his house at York. In the hall there were green say hangings and a long table. Identical hangings were to be found in the little parlour. In the great parlour there were hangings of diverse coloured say and a long table with a carpet. The furniture of the great chamber was more elaborate. Here the hangings were of overseas work, one part silk and the other with worked images. There was a Turkey carpet and carpets for the windows (presumably for the window seats) and for the forms and chairs. There was a hanging of Arras in the bedchamber.

The chapel was furnished at much more expense. It had hangings of tawny satin. There were two or three satin cushions and a vestment of the same material. There was also an Arras hanging worked with a picture of Our Lord and of St Mary Magdalen. There were three altar cloths, a Mass book, another vestment and two cruets of silver and gilt.

There were some household effects at Beverley and hangings with the story of St Catherine in the chapel there. At Cherry Burton there were two carts. Some stuffs were noted in the house at York and two silver basins for shaving in the pantry and much goodly diaper. It is added in a final note that there were also some hogsheads of Claret, brought from Hull to York, and some silver flagons and silver spoons.

Admittedly the large accommodation and also probably the silver were part of the appurtenances of an elderly priest with an assured position in the ecclesiastical administration of the archdiocese of York, but for the rest these details suggest in a very general way the background of the secular clergy.

Other elements of their life are suggested in a recent study[1] of the secular priesthood of the diocese of Lincoln, at that time the largest of the English bishoprics. It included Lincolnshire and Rutland and the whole of what would be the hunting counties and then, in the South, Oxfordshire, Buckinghamshire and Bedfordshire. It stretched from the ferries across the Humber to the passage of the Thames at Wallingford. At this time there were auxiliary bishops in the southern half of the diocese, Augustine Church, Abbot of Thame and after his death in 1514 Roger Smyth, Abbot of Dorchester. Both prelates held in succession the titular see of Lydda in Palestine.

In one respect the case of Lincoln was quite unusual for it had the University of Oxford within its borders. In 1520 the presentation of graduates to livings[2] in the diocese amounted to eleven per cent of the total. It was the non-graduates who may be held to represent the general body of the secular clergy. The graduates in this analysis were those who had obtained their mastership and among the non-graduates there was a proportion who had spent some time in the university. The greater part of the priesthood seems to have come from the grammar schools or, in the case of the Lincoln diocese, from education at chantries like those at Burghersh and Buckingham.[3]

As for the books in their possession, only scanty evidence is available. They seem to have varied between the copy of the *Summa Angelica* presented by William Smith, Rector of Belton to the Carthusians[4] at Axholme to the devotional works which were sold at a penny at John Dorne's bookshop[5] at Oxford. The references to books in wills are fragmentary and occasional and none was mentioned among Archdeacon Dalby's possessions. The Vicar of Easton Neston, who held that parish for nearly thirty years, bequeathed his book of sermons to the prior of the Blackfriars at Northampton.[6]

Perhaps further research may show that the body of the secular

---

[1] Margaret Bowker, *The Secular Clergy in the Diocese of Lincoln 1495–1520* (1968).
[2] *ibid.*, p. 45.   [3] *ibid.*, p. 51.   [4] *ibid.*, p. 52.
[5] Cf. *The Day Book of John Dorne*, ed. C. R. L. Fletcher, Oxford Historical Society (1885), V, p. 71 ff.   [6] Bowker, *op. cit.*, p. 54.

Moor Ld Chancelour

7 Sir Thomas More

8 Thomas Cromwell

clergy were more 'static' than has been imagined. Although, unlike those of the Tridentine Church, they were not tied in any way to their diocese of origin their opportunities for movement were probably restricted. In the case of the Lincoln diocese, many presentations were made by the Prior of St John of Jerusalem in England and by the abbots of the great houses of St Albans and Ramsey.

It does not seem at present clear who benefited by these presentations and at the same time some associations of secular clergy in the Lincoln diocese are left unmentioned. Thus at Stonor, near Henley, at the southern end of the jurisdiction there had been a long established chantry[1] dating back to 1349 and consisting of six chaplains. One of these became later the Stonors' chantry priest at Horton Kirby and another was presented to the benefice of Chipping Ilsley by the Prior of St John of Jerusalem in England. It is worth noting that Sir Adrian Fortescue, who resided much of his life at Stonor Park, was a member of this Order. The last reference to the six chaplains acting together is at the funeral of Lady Anne Fortescue in 1518. It is not possible to pursue this matter for, as far as the subject of this book is concerned, the secular clergy are only considered in the degree that their lives impinged upon those who formed King Henry's Court.

Other instances will confirm the customs of the time. One example is worth giving in some detail. According to the will of Sir John Skevington,[2] alderman of London and merchant of the staple of Calais, dated 31 December 1524, he bequeathed to the parish church of Skevington, where he was born, a vestment with his arms on the cross; to the church of Our Lady of Bradley in Lincolnshire, a white damask vestment with the like arms; to the Grey, Black, Augustine and White Friars the sum of £81 to pray for his soul and to bring his body back to burial. The remainder of the candles used at his burials to be divided between St Mary Woolnoth and the Crutched Friars to burn before the glorious Sacrament and on Corpus Christi Day. At the death of Sir Thomas Lovell,[3] Knight of the Garter and speaker of the House of Com-

---

[1] Cf. R. J. Stonor, *Stonor* (1951), pp. 365–7.
[2] *Letters and Papers, Henry VIII*, 1523–5, p. 412.
[3] *Letters and Papers, Henry VIII*, 1525–6, p. 154.

mons, the sum of £10 was left as offering to the priest who would say a *De Profundis* at his tomb daily for a year.

There were arrangements for the payment of a stipend to a chaplain to reside with young Lord Monteagle at Sleaford,[1] presumably to complete his education. This was part of Lord Hussey's attempt to secure him as a son-in-law. A list of the stuff and plate at the Chapel Royal[2] shows, 'Two rich Arras pieces of the Kings of Collen [Cologne]. Two Arras pieces of the Assumption and the Salutation. Two of white damask with the Salutation and roses crowned.' A final note is added. 'Cloth of gold with roses and columbine.'

A survey of the testamentary dispositions has a bearing mainly on the practice of the great old stocks and their dependents. Thus Lord Mountjoy, the father of the Marchioness of Exeter, arranged[3] that he should be buried in the chapel of Friars Minor in London 'where the body of my father is interred'. Lord Dudley[4] left his body to be buried in the priory of St James at Dudley and a thousand Masses to be said for his soul. Margaret, Duchess of Norfolk, the first Duke's widow, instructed[5] her executors to find 300 priests secular and religious, to say 300 Masses and *diriges* for her soul within ten days of her decease. The Marquess of Berkeley willed[6] that the White Friars should sing perpetually in their church in Fleet Street, in the suburbs of London at the altar of St Gascon, for the repose of his soul and for those of his father, mother, niece, and his son, Sir Thomas Berkeley, for evermore.

The first Marquess of Dorset asked[7] that 100 Masses be said for him at each of the churches of the four Orders of Friars in London. There was a good deal of attachment to the Dominicans.[8] Lord Vaux and his stepson Sir Thomas Parr[9] both left instructions for their burial in the London Blackfriars if they died within that area. Vaux arranged to be buried in the church at Harrowden, if he died within the county of Northampton.

Many of these bequests, and especially the more elaborate, have

---

[1] *ibid.*, p. 416.
[2] *Letters and Papers, Henry VIII*, 1526–8, p. 1384.
[3] *Testamenta Vetusta*, vol. II, ed. Nicholas Harvis Nicolas (1826), p. 386.
[4] *ibid.*, p. 391.   [5] *ibid.*, p. 404.   [6] *ibid.*, p. 408.   [7] *ibid.*, p. 442.
[8] Cf. for other instances *ibid.*, pp. 434 and 490.
[9] *ibid.*, pp. 548 and 600. Sir Thomas Parr was the father of Queen Catherine.

probably something of the conventional; but there are three among them which have an element of pathos for they show so marked a confidence that the existing order would endure. The first is that of Lord Dinham[1] of Car Dinham, a great landowner in Cornwall and Western Devonshire, Warden of the Stannaries and Keeper of Dartmoor Forest, one of the chief supporters of the Courtenay family. He left his body to be buried in the Abbey of Hartland if he died within a hundred miles of that house, which he had founded, otherwise in the Greyfriars in London.

The other two[2] relate to members of the country gentry. Sir Thomas Wyndham of Felbrigg left Masses with prayers to Our Redeemer, to his Blessed Mother, to St John the Evangelist, St George, St Thomas of Canterbury, St Margaret, St Catherine and St Barbara [his titular patrons]. Sir Ralph Shirley gave moneys for the finding and upholding of a lamp 'to burn continually day and night before the Blessed Sacrament in the parish church of Rakedale in Leicestershire for evermore'.

[1] *ibid.*, p. 496.   [2] *ibid.*, pp. 542 and 581.

PART TWO

CROMWELL'S EPOCH

I

Hans Holbein

Hans Holbein, through whose eyes we see the figures of King Henry's Court, came to England in the winter of 1526. He was born in Augsburg in 1497 and was already a painter of distinction. He lived for some years in Basel and had undertaken painting on walls and organ doors, altar pieces and sacred pictures which were the custom of his time.

He had, however, already established his reputation as a portrait painter. His head-and-shoulders of Erasmus had been sent to England to show his quality. He had already painted the remarkable heads of Benedikt von Herberstein and Bonifacius Amerbach[1] and in 1526 he had just finished what is now known as the Darmstadt Madonna. In this picture the Blessed Virgin is seen guarding with her cloak the Meyer family, the father Jakob kneeling at her feet and beside him his two young sons. The background is a reddish marble and grey stone set within a shell-shaped niche supported by the carved pilasters of two columns. His talent and his settings were both matured before he came to England.

He travelled on the recommendations of Erasmus, then living near him at Basel. He went from the Rhine Gate of his city and down the length of that great river and across the Rhineland. It seems that he took shipping at Antwerp, where he may have met Quentin Maatsys, and thus came to London. He had three periods in this country. The first was centred on the hospitality and began with the patronage of Sir Thomas More. In 1528 he returned to Basel and came back to England in 1532. Five years later he again went abroad and visited Basel; but on New Year's Day 1539 he was again in London and remained there until he died of the

[1] Painted respectively in 1517 and 1519.

plague in the late autumn of 1543. He was only just forty-six years old. He came fully equipped and worked with speed; it is wonderful what he accomplished in these few years.

One evidently knows little of his personal ideas, but it seems natural to conceive him as a disciple of Erasmus, his friend and patron. Thus he seems to have been too close to the monasteries of Basel, his adopted city, to appreciate their inmates. There were certain disputes[1] about the retention of his father's painting materials by the monks of the Antonian Abbey of Isenheim. The altar piece that he painted for the charterhouse of Val Sainte Marguerite found no parallel in his work in England. He had, for whatever reason, a very clear detachment from the religious disputes of his period in the northern kingdom.

It has always seemed to me that his talent was for understanding the successful man of business of his time, whether they were the merchants of Basel, or of the London Steelyard, or the great predatory figures of King Henry's Court. These were essentially the men who, behind a certain bravura in their adornment, concealed the determination and the secret life of those who gain great new resources. In England it was especially those men who saw in the monastic lands a welcome and an unexpected harvest.

Of course there are various ways of examining Holbein's outlook and his first English portraits, due to the patronage of Thomas More, were very different from those which I have just described. He was at his very best in dealing with men who had reached or were coming towards maturity. His few paintings of youths, such as that of Sir Thomas More's son John, appear insipid. He was not, I think, very interested in painting women. There is a sort of dulled-over charm which can be seen perhaps especially in the young girls of the More household. He has been credited, and surely with justice, with an extreme truthfulness and exactness and one feels that he tells us all that we can need to know about the King's third wife Jane Seymour, or the Princess of Cleves. He was a German with German standards and perhaps the Princess of Cleves was more pleasing to him than to English tastes.

The French were for the most part beyond his sympathy and he

---

[1] For a description of this episode cf. A. B. Chamberlain, *Hans Holbein the Younger* (1913), I, pp. 13–15.

could not be imagined as painting the great mistresses of Francis I, the Duchesses of Etampes and Valentinois, any more than the ruffling French generals. This is another way of saying that *panache* was outside his ken. It is not surprising that Philip Melancthon is the one German Reformer whose portrait by Holbein has come down to us; Holbein was, perhaps, taken by the Erasmian side of his character.

The portraits of ecclesiastics were like the altar pieces, something concerned with the period of his youth. Those like Archbishop Warham and Bishop Fisher and the portrait of a young priest,[1] once called John Colet, arose from his contacts with Thomas More. They were not repeated in his later life.[2] It was his good fortune to be interested in the portrayal of acquisitive men at a period when the leaders of the English Court were most longsighted and acquisitive. Those who could have seen his earliest portraits, those of Benedikt von Herberstein and Bonifacius Amerbach, both the heirs of Basel patricians engaged upon the money market, would have known what to expect from this great portrait painter.

Holbein's first visit to England was to Sir Thomas More, not to the Court and this prevented him from coming within the field of Cardinal Wolsey's patronage. The conception of a portrait painter had so far hardly crossed the King's horizon and the painters in attendance were employed chiefly in the decoration of wall spaces and in those works which were associated with the Cloth of Gold. Two of More's friends,[3] Sir John Gage who appealed to him as a Catholic and Sir Thomas Eliot who was linked with him as a humanist, were subjects of Holbein's early portraits; but his chief work was his great set-piece of the More family and the individual heads associated with it.

It is supposed to have been commissioned for Sir Thomas's fiftieth birthday and a carefully drawn pen sketch was conveyed to Erasmus and thence to the museum at Basel. The original picture is now lost. Among the best copies is that at Nostell Priory which

[1] Reproductions of these portraits face pp. 64, 65, 97.
[2] These comments are not invalidated by the existence of the portrait of Georges de Selve Bishop of Lavaur in 'The Ambassadors'.
[3] These portraits are reproduced facing pp. 97, 112.

seems to incorporate some of Holbein's work. It seems probable that the original picture was completed and was that which was found in the Arundel Collection and passed later to the Bishop of Olmutz. This version may have been destroyed in a fire at the palace of Kremsier in 1752.

The main interest of the picture is derived from the intimate details that are preserved. The scene was apparently set in the dining-hall of More's house in Chelsea, although there are no trestles set out for a meal. There is a porch of open woodwork, which projects into the room. A window with lattices is indicated and upon its sill a jug, a candlestick and some books. On the left there is a sideboard carrying a flower vase, tankards and silver plate. It is too early for the figures to be arranged as a true conversation-piece. Lady More has a chained monkey by her side. In the Nostell Priory picture two dogs are introduced, a 'Bologna shock' at Sir Thomas's feet and a 'cur dog' beside his father, Sir John. In the original pen sketch a clock hangs on the wall above Sir Thomas's head and there are nine members of his family around him.

There are certain pictures from Holbein's first period in England which do not fit into any convenient scheme. Thus from one angle Sir Nicholas Carew was an associate of Sir Thomas More, and Sir Henry Guldeford[1] and Sir Bryan Tuke had some connections with him. None of the three can be considered, in the true sense, within his circle. It is difficult to place Reskimer, 'a Cornish gentleman'. Niklaus Kratzer, the astronomer, was a compatriot and a friend of Holbein's. I am not aware of any contacts with either More or Holbein of the two Godsalves, Thomas and Sir John.[2]

It has naturally been extremely difficult to discover both the scope and the details of Holbein's work. Unlike the eighteenth-century painters there is in his case no correspondence with private patrons and, of course, no order-book. At the same time the fact that for a hundred years there was no portraitist in England of his own reputation has led to the preservation of some material and there is nothing more valuable than the great book of Holbein's

---

[1] The drawing of Sir Henry Guldeford is reproduced, facing p. 112.
[2] The portraits of Mr Reskimer and Sir John Godsalve are reproduced facing p. 113.

drawings,[1] now broken up, which was found by Queen Caroline in a bureau in Kensington Palace in 1727. Besides the drawings for most of the extant Holbein portraits, the volume also contained several for pictures which were either never painted or have since disappeared. The drawings are eighty-seven in number and include four portraits which were not by Holbein. Those which are attributed to him include eighteen of which the subjects have not yet been identified and are probably for the most part unidentifiable. It seems correct to state that they all relate to portraits painted in England and that they are continued until the end of Holbein's life.

In one way the drawings give a more accurate picture of the great Tudor functionaries than do the completed paintings. The features stand out more clearly than do those in which attention is distracted to the elaborate decoration of the richly coloured clothing. In his second visit Holbein would have another advantage. By that time More's circle had broken up and he would now find as his subjects those who were the chosen instruments of the King's new policies. These were the crucial years in which to study the evolution of the sovereign's courtiers.

[1] *The Drawings of Holbein at Windsor Castle* was published in 1945 by K. T. Parker, who provides an admirable introduction on this subject, pp. 7–34.

II

The Tranquil Years

If the English scene alone is considered, the years that followed on the Cloth of Gold were very tranquil. The fall of the Duke of Buckingham must have seemed a single episode; there was no one else about the Court who now possessed that strange hang-over from the high fifteenth-century aristocracy. One of the old-time christenings had recently taken place, that of the Lady Frances 'first-begotten daughter of Charles Duke of Suffolk and the Queen of France'.[1] The road to the church at Bishop's Hatfield was strewn with rushes; the church porch was hung with cloth of gold and needlework. Within the church were deep panels of Arras describing the histories of Hercules and Holofernes. In the chancel was an Arras of silk and gold. The altar was covered with a rich cloth of tissue and placed on it were images and relics, all set with jewels. Lady Boleyn[2] and Lady Elizabeth Grey were deputies for the godmothers, the Queen of England and the Princess Mary. The Abbot of St Albans was the godfather. The child, who later became the Marchioness of Dorset and the mother of Lady Jane Grey, received the name of Frances for she was born upon the feast of St Francis of Assisi.

The links with the Continent were very close. The King corresponded with the Duke of Ferrara asking him to take back into favour John Galeazzo Boschetto, secretary to the Cardinal of Agen, who had unconsciously offended him. He was highly recommended by the English King's secretary for Latin Letters. In return[3] the Duke sent to the King an Italian lute. At the same

---

[1] *Letters and Papers, Henry VIII*, 1515–8, no. 1108.
[2] Presumably Lady Elizabeth Boleyn, mother of the future Queen Anne.
[3] *Letters and Papers*, nos. 1081 and 1178.

time Mgre de Rossi wrote[1] that the Pope having raised him to be a Cardinal-Elect, he hoped that he should not be wanting in gratitude towards his benefactor. If King Henry desired to make use of him for his affairs, he hoped that he would be found equal in diligence to His Grace's many other servants at the Court of Rome.

In these years there was no hesitation about borrowings from Italy. In March 1519 there occurred a note of the expenses of a revel, called a 'maskalyne' after the manner of Italy. And in the same year Dr Pace wrote to the Cardinal from Cologne 'remembering the Italian proverb that it is good some time to set a candle afore the devil'.[2]

At the same time the financial contacts went on smoothly. Thus Thomas Cardinal Archbishop of York and Lord Chancellor borrowed[3] in the King's name a matter of £24,000 from a *consortium* of seventeen Italian men of business headed by Leonard Frescobaldi, merchant of Florence and Anthony Cavalari, merchant of Lucca. John Frescobaldi was their representative at the London end. On a more private level James Fugger of Augsburg wrote[4] to Sir Robert Wingfield that he had not received the repayment of six thousand florins, which had become due on the 17th of the previous month.

It was at about this time that Cardinal Campeggio first appears upon the scene as a correspondent. He had been sent to England on a mission to incite the King to join with other Christian princes in a crusade against the Turks. Later in April 1520 he had written[5] to Wolsey describing the rising power of Cardinal Santi Quattro and in the next month he drew attention to the low standing of the nuncios that the Pope was now sending, to England, the Bishop of Ascoli and to the Emperor, Mariano Caraccioli, a protonotary apostolic.

The view of the Court of Rome was much foreshortened. Thus Campeggio would write[6] of the determination of Francis I to

---

[1] *ibid.*, no. 1092.　　[2] *Letters and Papers, 1519–21*, p. 91.
[3] *Letters and Papers, 1515–18*, no. 950.
[4] *ibid.*, letter dated 3 January 1517, no. 882.
[5] The Cardinal Priest of the Santi Quattro Incoronati, *Letters and Papers, Henry VIII, 1515–18*, p. 268.
[6] *Letters and Papers, 1519–21*, p. 360.

secure the promotion of Monseigneur de Longueville to the cardinalate and of his opposition to that of Erard de la Marck, the
Imperialist Bishop of Liège. The same flat impression is conveyed
in the news sent back[1] from Rome by agents in the English service.
'The Pope has taken a fever. He is very corpulent and full of ill
humours which cause apprehension.' The same week a letter
came[2] from Ghent for Cardinal Wolsey asking him to secure that
the writer's brother, the Bishop of Maurienne, should receive a
Hat at the next creation. This correspondence perhaps conveyed
an over-emphasis on Wolsey's power. After all one does not obtain
a clear impression of Pope Leo X from all these letters. To both the
English Cardinal and his sovereign Italy was a foreign land,
which they had never visited.

Among the letters of this time is one from Sir William Fitzwilliam to the King. He was at this time Vice-Admiral of England.
In 1521 he had just returned from a mission to France. 'It fortuned,' he explained,[3] 'that [at the French Court] they well per-
ceived that he that taught me was a master; which I showed them
was Your Grace.' This is an instance of the approach of those who
would become the King's intimate servants. It was the character
of these men that they came to Court quite young and kept very
close. Fitzwilliam became in time Earl of Southampton and Lord
Admiral of England.

A good impression of the movements of the Court can be obtained from the applications which followed the death from the
plague of Sir William Compton, who left no adult heir to carry on
the duties of his many offices. The applications naturally went
through the hands of the Cardinal of York. Sir George Throckmorton, the head of a family which was now making forward
drew[4] the Cardinal's attention to his claims to the sheriffdom of
Worcestershire and the office of *custos rotulorum* of Warwickshire.
He also saw fit to mention the vacant stewardship of the see of
Worcester, a post which had the more importance because between 1497 and 1535 this bishopric was held *in commendam* by a
series of non-resident Italian prelates. He also mentioned hopefully
that the office of under-treasurer of England was likewise vacant.

[1] *ibid.*, p. 348.   [2] *ibid.*, p. 348.   [3] *ibid.*, p. 433.
[4] *Letters and Papers, Henry VIII, 1527-8*, p. 1962.

There was also a letter from the Duke of Richmond,[1] who was already established in his northern fortress. He was nine years old and his advisers must have thought out the letter sent in his name to his royal father. In this he asked for the promotion of Sir Giles Strangeways and Sir Edward Seymour, 'the master of my horse', to posts left vacant by Sir William's death. He drew attention to the stewardship of Canford. In the next month came a letter[2] from the Countess of Salisbury asking for a grant of Canford. She contended that the profits of this lordship were part and parcel of her earldom; but that Sir William Compton had persuaded the King that they belonged to the lands of the duchy of Somerset. There was also another letter[3] from Sir George Throckmorton to Thomas Cromwell, asking for his influence with the Lord Cardinal's Grace.

In August 1528 a division was made[4] of the late Sir William's offices. Henry Jerningham, steward to the Princess Mary, became Constable of Gloucester Castle. Walter Walshe, page of the Privy Chamber received the post of constable and keeper of Elmley Castle. Sir John Russell was appointed as steward, surveyor, receiver and bailiff of the lordship of Stoke under Hampden and Cory Malet.

The King was very fearful of the plague and during these years it was the sickness that kept him so often out of London. It was a consequence of mobility of the well-to-do that there were so few plague victims among the gentry. In this respect Sir William Compton's death was quite unusual.

The King was not accustomed to seek hospitality from his subjects. This was a practice that was to come in with Queen Elizabeth, but he used the royal manors and the old royal castles. It is not suggested that there was accommodation for the courtiers in these small houses like Easthampstead and Woodstock and old Richmond palace. There was also Beaulieu in Essex, which he used and then gave up. In this connection one cannot forget Wolsey's great house at Hampton Court or York House, which was of a moderate size, or the Moor, which was quite a little place. It seems that the King would use them all and very soon would reassume their ownership.

[1] ibid., p. 1980.   [2] ibid., p. 2023.   [3] ibid., p. 2016.   [4] ibid., pp. 2034–5.

The privy council expenses[1] for the first half of 1530 throw some
light on the circle within which Henry moved before the religious
changes broke upon the nation. Among the givers of presents were
the heads of monastic houses, while to parallel this there were the
alms on the royal journeys, to the friars of Hounslow and to a
hermit met upon the way. A White Friar received a gift of 100
crowns. There were gifts to a servant of Lord Berkeley's for bringing a fresh sturgeon, and to a man from Lady Sydney with orange
pies. A fresh salmon was brought in by the men of Staines.

It was now the height of summer. The Provost of Eton's servant
came with cakes. The gardener of Beaulieu brought strawberries
to the King. The gardeners of York Place came with cherries,
those of Hampton Court brought pears and damsons and from
Richmond came damascenes. A considerable sum was paid to the
keeper of the clock at Hampton Court and some £15 to Vincent
the Painter for trimming the King's new barge. This was Vincenzo
Vulpe. It is clear that the King felt that his talents should be thus
channelled. Mr Fitzwilliam was Treasurer of the Household, a
strong persistent courtier. There are two references to the King's
dogs who had got lost. Cut, the King's spaniel, was re-discovered
and Ball, the King's dog, was brought home after he had been lost
in Waltham Forest. This is the point at which we should consider
the entry on the scene of the Duke of Richmond.

In the last part of the winter of 1519 at a date which cannot be
defined exactly Elizabeth Blount, one of the young maids of
honour to the Queen, Catherine of Aragon, gave birth to a son in
the house called Jericho, which was the residence of the Augustinian prior at Blackmore in Essex. The child was christened Henry
and surnamed Fitzroy; he was the eldest son of the King. His godfather was the Cardinal, who made all arrangements for him, he
was brought up in his immediate care.

His mother came from one of the spreading branches of the
Blount family. Her distant relative Lord Mountjoy, the Queen's
Chamberlain, was trustee of her parents' marriage settlement.
She was thus a remote cousin and contemporary of Gertrude
Blount, who had a defined but small place in the reign as Mar-
chioness of Exeter. Her parents, who were still young, were Sir

---

[1] *Letters and Papers, Henry VIII*, vol. V.

9 Duke of Norfolk

10 An Ecclesiastic

11 Sir John Gage

John Blount of Kinlet in Shropshire and Catherine, daughter of Sir Hugh Peshall,[1] who had joined Henry VII at Bosworth Field in the train of his friend and relative, the Earl of Derby.

The King was devoted to religious observance. He heard three Masses on hunting days and five Masses at other times. There is no indication that he ever returned to Mistress Blount; he left her in the custody of the Cardinal. This was one of the sides of the royal character which was incomprehensible to that cheerful *roué*, the King of France.

In some ways this event seems to have had a similar effect on the marriage of King Henry and Catherine that the birth of a son to Marie Walewska had on the marriage of the Emperor Napoleon and Josephine. It seems that all his life the child Lord Henry Fitzroy, as he was at first known, retained a grateful and loving admiration for his tremendous father. These were the years in which the Cardinal was all-in-all to his young master.

This was also the last happy period for Queen Catherine. Since 1521 her only child the Princess Mary had been betrothed to the Emperor and she does not appear to have considered the difficulty of expecting her nephew to remain unmarried until her daughter had reached maturity. The complication of extracting himself from this engagement was got over by the Emperor's statement that the dowry had not yet been paid, nor had the princess been sent to Spain for her education. In consequence, in 1525 he freed himself and married instead the Princess of Portugal. King Henry began to lose interest in his daughter and at the same time he decided to advance his only son.

It was in the summer of 1525 that King Henry, still acting in close contact with the Cardinal, proceeded to promote his little boy. Lord Henry Fitzroy was then six years of age. On 7 June he was elected a Knight of the Garter and, before his installation three weeks later, was raised both to an earldom and a dukedom. He already kept his household at Durham Place. The description of the ceremony is very detailed. It took place in the Presence Chamber at the palace of Bridewell. This chamber was approached

---

[1] Such details as can be discovered about Elizabeth Blount and her relations are gathered together by their descendant William Childs-Pemberton in *Elizabeth Blount and Henry VIII* (1913).

G

from the new gallery hung with tapestries of the Fall of Troy. At the end of the chamber was a cloth of estate and under this a chair of gold tissue with the pommels of the royal chair gilded with fine gold. Beside the King on his right hand stood the Cardinal Legate.

Lord Henry came in to receive his earldom led by the Earls of Arundel and Oxford. He then retired and returned supported by the Duke of Norfolk and the Duke of Suffolk. He was created Duke of Richmond and Somerset and Earl of Nottingham and took his place beside the King above all other peers. The King's nephew Henry, son and heir of the Duke of Suffolk was carried in and created Earl of Lincoln. Two other relatives were raised in rank, the Earl of Devon becoming Marquess of Exeter and Lord Roos, Earl of Rutland. As a foretaste of the future, Sir Thomas Boleyn was advanced to the peerage as Viscount Rochford.

By the end of July the Duke had been created Lord High Admiral of England, Wales, Ireland, Normandy, Gascony and Aquitaine; this office was for life. He also received the post of Warden General of all the Marches towards Scotland. Sheriff Hutton Castle was assigned as the headquarters of this new administration. The Dean of the Duke's Chapel was the Archdeacon of Richmond. Archdeacon Magnus was surveyor and receiver general and Sir William Bulmer steward of his household. Lands were granted to him across England including Sheriff Hutton, Sutton-upon-Derwent and many other Yorkshire manors. Tattershall and East and West Deeping in Lincolnshire, Thorpe Waterville in Bedfordshire, Bassingbourne in Cambridgeshire, Cheshunt in Hertfordshire, Bedhampton in Hampshire, Corfe Castle and Canford in Dorsetshire, Curry Revell, Carnell *Reginae* and Langport in Somerset, Bovey Tracy and Sampford Peveril in Devon, Dartford in Kent and Kirby-in-Kendal in Westmorland, Dalby in Derbyshire, Ridlington in Rutland, Dartwith in Worcestershire, Walsall in Staffordshire and Bishop's Lynn in Norfolk. There were also two manors in Pembrokeshire and two in Cardigan. These are just a selection. The King was generous with the possessions of the White Rose royal house; he was still carving up the widespread lands of the late Duke of Buckingham.

These promotions produced a painful effect upon Queen

Catherine. She had been used to the bastards of the House of Aragon, who never usurped the royal titles, and the revival of her father-in-law's earldom of Richmond as a dukedom for her husband's bastard son seemed a threat to the position of her daughter. There is no clear evidence upon this matter, but it seems likely that the King and Cardinal both toyed with the idea that if the Queen had no further children the succession might in time pass to his bastard son.

These were the years, too, when a royal marriage, perhaps with a Princess of Portugal, was under consideration for the little boy. And this could only have been brought about for him by some established place in the succession to the throne.

The young Duke had his household moved up into Yorkshire. He would go to Sheriff Hutton, where the late Duke of Norfolk had been living. The whole region had Yorkist memories. Sheriff Hutton Castle towered over the small town. Its high windows faced southward across the plain of York. A chapel elaborately furnished was provided there by Wolsey.[1] This was because Lord Darcy and Lord Latimer both had chapels in their own houses.

Gifts were exchanged with his young cousin, King James V; bloodhounds were sent to him from Scotland. There was a correspondence with his father, who sent him north a lute. In return came suitable quotations from Caesar's *Commentaries*. There were gifts from Lord Northumberland and presents to the Countess of Westmorland on the christening of her heir. The gentlemen of the North appeared to visit him, the two Sir Marmaduke Constables, father and son. His *entourage* was not entirely composed of priests and greybeards. There was Sir Edward Seymour, a name to watch, as master of the horse. There were the Duke's young uncles, still almost boys, George and William Blount; the former was one of the Duke of Norfolk's many wards.

The Duke's mother was in the Cardinal's care and in these years she was married to Sir Gilbert Tailboys of Kyme in Lincolnshire, who was in his household. He was raised to the peerage and died quite soon. An offer was then made to her by Lord Leonard Grey, but she preferred the young Lord Clinton, some years her junior.

[1] *Letters and Papers*, vol. IV, p. 393.

When autumn came, the Duke and his household moved south to the royal castle of Pontefract, towards the southern borders of his jurisdiction. He had command of all the forces to the north of Trent.

III

Anne Boleyn

Anne Boleyn was a determined woman. With a strain of hardness in her character and with her education at the Court of France she was not likely to conciliate the ladies of the English Court. She seems to have understood her uncle the Duke of Norfolk and likewise placed no reliance on her time-serving father, Sir Thomas Boleyn. She had a warm and devoted affection for her brother George, later Lord Rochford, who was a few years younger than herself. With very little assistance from their numerous relatives, they made their way together.

She was born in 1502 or 1503.[1] She is sometimes confused with her sister Mary; but I prefer Dr Friedmann's reading of the chronology[2] to that of Dr Gairdner. She probably entered the service of the Queen of France on the marriage of King Henry's sister in 1514; there is no purpose in suggesting that she went in 1521, when her father was ambassador. She and Lady Elizabeth Grey were left behind because as little girls they could not exercise that foreign influence, which all the Courts of Europe then so much dreaded. Her subsequent training was in the hands of Queen Claude, the first wife of Francis I.

Her period in France had marked her strongly; it formed part of her technique in her approach to her own sovereign. It affected those young men by whom in time she was surrounded. It gave her an almost Gallic realism. It has never been suggested that she was beautiful. She had a slender figure, a long neck and lovely black hair. In the days of her glory she liked to wear this loose

---

[1] For a discussion on this matter see Paul Friedmann's *Anne Boleyn* (1884), vol. II, pp. 313–22. The *D.N.B.* gives her date of birth unequivocally as 1507.
[2] Cf. Friedmann, *op. cit.*, p. 318 and pp. 323–7.

with diamonds in it. One finger was malformed. She had sparkling eyes, well-fitted to awake concupiscence.

It is curious that she did not marry. In 1522, when she returned to England, there had been a project of marriage with her cousin Sir James Butler, the eldest son of the eighth Earl of Ormonde and in the subsequent years Sir Henry Percy, the Earl of Northumberland's eldest son, had wished to marry her. This was prevented by Cardinal Wolsey. It is possible that the dowry offered with her was not attractive. Her father was himself a younger son. Sir Thomas Boleyn was in some respects a curious figure.[1] He was timorous and parsimonious and in every way a perfect courtier. He would never be drawn into taking any risks. In his early life he had benefited from the advice of the Duke of Norfolk, whose sister Lady Elizabeth Howard he had married in those grim years when her House had suffered an eclipse. It may be said that he would be faithful to his daughter so long as she continued to please the King. There was his lodestar.

Anne Boleyn was not herself in any way opposed to the old Catholic atmosphere. So far as she had any preferences these seem to have been for the negligent practice of the Court of France. The picture that the Spaniards in time formed of the Lutheran 'Ana Bolena' was not realistic in any way.

Three phases marked the period between the beginning of King Henry's attraction to her and her royal marriage. Her religious attitude, if this may be so called, was dictated to her by the presence of Queen Catherine as the King's wife. She was early determined to avoid the position of a royal mistress. The King, partly on account of his devotion to religious practices, was most inconstant; he was never kind to those he took as mistresses. There had been the cases of Elizabeth Blount, now Lady Tailboys, and that of Anne's sister Mary. Mary was particularly unfortunate for she had yielded to the sovereign when already a married woman and the wife of William Carey, one of the gentlemen of the King's chamber. She had gained nothing by this brief connection; it was only Sir Thomas Boleyn who then made forward.

Each of the phases showed her firm resistance to the King's desires. During the first phase it appears that Cardinal Wolsey did

---

[1] Cf. Holbein's drawing, reproducing facing p. 128.

not realize the situation. As his actions towards Elizabeth Blount had shown, the Cardinal had a somewhat *bourgeois* attitude towards his sovereign. He held that the King should only marry within the blood royal with the object of building up a framework of alliance. His relations with Queen Catherine were strained and he hoped that if that marriage might be annulled the King would choose a French princess. When King Henry's new attachment was made clear to him, there followed an uneasy situation in which the King and Cardinal worked together at the Court of Rome to secure an annulment which would enable Henry VIII to marry Anne Boleyn. In the later portion of this period there emerged the figure of Stephen Gardiner, who was much the ablest of the King's ecclesiastical advisers.

During the second phase the King and his *inamorata* had turned against the Cardinal. Anne Boleyn had emerged as a political force in her own right. For a time she had beside her all those varied politicians who wished to break up and to end the period of Cardinal Wolsey's rule. These were the few years in which the Duke of Norfolk, for his own ends, was closest to her.

It was followed by the third phase when she was once again in isolation. Her *insouciance* had turned the Duke of Suffolk and still more his wife, the King's sister, against her. Stephen Gardiner, who had received the bishopric of Winchester, now withdrew from her. The men of the official world, for example Fitzwilliam and Guldeford, were secretly her enemies. She could rely only on a single element, her powers to fascinate the King.

Meanwhile, there was the whole business of what is often called the Divorce, but was in reality the proposed annulment of Queen Catherine's marriage; it was this which in time brought the Cardinal down. In detail this subject has been much worked over[1] and except in outline it remains remote from the lives of the King's courtiers. One difficulty was caused by the opposition of the Queen's nephew the Emperor at the Holy See. A Legatine Court was set up in 1529 with Wolsey and Cardinal Campeggio, who had been sent to England for this purpose, as legates. Its sittings at the great hall of the Black Friars lasted through the months of May to July when the recess was ordered by Campeggio according to

[1] For a modern study cf. G. de C. Parmiter, *The King's Great Matter* (1967).

Roman practice, and Pope Clement at the same time called the case to Rome.

An inner circle of the elder courtiers was called upon for depositions connected with the married life of Queen Catherine long ago in 1501 and 1502 in London and at Ludlow. It is noticeable that such were not asked from avowed supporters of the Queen, like Lady Salisbury. These notes, which in character are rather heavy and are all concerned with this one matter, will serve to show the degree to which the courtiers were concerned with the King's question. Evidence was first sought from three persons of distinction, Lords Shrewsbury and Dorset and Sir Anthony Willoughby.[1]

George Earl of Shrewsbury stated that he was now fifty-nine years of age. At night (in 1501) he with my Lord of Oxford and others had conducted Prince Arthur to the Lady Catherine's bedchamber and left him there. He supposed that the Prince had consummated the marriage as he himself had done being only fifteen and a half at his own wedding. The Marquess of Dorset, giving his age as fifty-two, said that he believed the Prince Arthur had used the Princess as his wife for he was of a good and sanguine complexion. Sir Anthony Willoughby explained that he had lived fifteen years in Hampshire and another twelve in Wiltshire. By the favour of his father, Lord Broke, steward of the King's household, he was present when the Prince went to bed on his marriage night in the Bishop of London's Palace. In the morning the Prince in the presence of Mr St John, Mr Crowne, Mr Griffith Rice *et alia* said to him, 'Willoughby, bring me a cup of ale for I have been this night in the midst of Spain.'

Some of the personal details have elements of interest. Thus Anthony Paynes and Sir William Thomas were now men of fifty. The first was born in Kent and had lived since then in the Isle of Wight and in Gloucestershire, the second was born in Carmarthen and had spent the last twenty-five years in the Marches. Both had served Prince Arthur long ago. Sir Henry Guldeford explained that he was forty, but could say nothing as to the matter of the consummation since he was then only twelve.

There was one clear statement on the other side. Nicholas West, Bishop of Ely gave his age as sixty-eight and said that he was pre-

[1] *Letters and Papers,* 1529, pp. 2579–82.

sent at the wedding. He could say nothing of the consummation, but that he doubted it. The Queen had often told him that she had not 'known' her husband, *quod non fuit carnaliter de dicto Arthuro cognita*. They were, however, both of sufficient age. There were details as to Sir David Owen of Cowdray in Sussex, who was reputed to be the stepbrother of Henry VII. He was stated to be born in Pembrokeshire and was now seventy. He had lived in England for forty years. Four peers connected with the Court gave an opinion. Lord Rochford, Anne Boleyn's father, believed that the marriage had been consummated; Lord Fitzwalter agreed with Lord Shrewsbury's judgement; Lord Darcy said that he had no direct evidence and Lord Mountjoy that at the time he had been too young to know. There is a certain familiarity in all these names.

There were two depositions from great ladies, both given later and in the country. Mary, wife of Henry Bourchier Earl of Essex and then forty-four years of age, declared that in her judgement the Prince and Princess had been man and wife. The statement of Agnes, widow of Thomas late Duke of Norfolk, was taken at Thetford by Sampson Michell in the presence of William Molyneux, her chaplain. She gave her age as fifty-two and over and said that Prince Arthur was about the stature of the young Earl of Derby, but not fully so high. She deposed that she had seen the Prince and Princess lying in the same bed in the Bishop of London's palace. Apart from these few depositions the great cause went forward without the intervention of the English Court.

These depositions throw some light upon this first marriage, as it was seen by the survivors of that time in the Court circle; but the case had been called away to Rome and the principal events that followed its recall were first the downfall and destruction of the great Cardinal and then the provision of what can best be described as a principal officer for the Church in England.

So many men conspired to bring Wolsey down; but it was the relentless pressure of Anne Boleyn which had most influence. She was a woman whose actions were unmeasured and this had something to do with her own fall; but for the present she had a single object to disembarrass the Court of the presence of the Cardinal.

In some ways Wolsey's position was stronger than that of any other English statesman of the period, for the reigning Pope, Clement VII, had appointed him to the legateship for life. There was also the fact that for years Henry had taken pleasure in the way in which the Cardinal of York had maintained his own prestige as a western king. Before the health of either broke they were both full-blooded men; for the first twenty years of this new reign the Cardinal had been an essential factor in the presentation of the English kingship. At first it would seem that the King was passive in the attack that now developed against Wolsey. In the previous months Wolsey had made use of the More, the name that he usually gave to Moore Park the country house that he occupied by right of his office as Abbot of St Albans. When charges were brought against him, he was instructed to go to Esher, an unfurnished house which belonged to him as Bishop of Winchester, a diocese which he had lately received in exchange for the see of Durham.

At this time he surrendered to the King the great palace that he had built at Hampton Court, constructed on land that he held leasehold for a term of years from the Knights of St John. He gave to the King he served the riches that had come to him. There was no personal ownership behind his splendour. He also with some difficulty gave to the King York House, which was the London residence of the northern primate. In these weeks he surrendered both the see of Winchester and the abbey of St Albans. He does not seem to have been too much cast down for he had only one enemy who was unreconcilable, Anne Boleyn. Perhaps he had some doubts as to the persistence of his sovereign's passion.

IV

The Rise of Cromwell

Looking back upon that time it now seems inevitable that it should have been Thomas Cromwell, arising from the wreck of Wolsey's fortunes, who should have emerged as the minister to serve his sovereign. He really had a working mind, a torrent of energy which could be used in his master's service. The others then in the public view who may have hoped to inherit the Cardinal's influence were, like the Duke of Norfolk, too grand to do the work that was required of them. The only answer was a man who came out from the Cardinal's stable.

There is much that is of great interest in Thomas Cromwell. He was a new man and a breaker of moulds. It was not that ministers in earlier times had not arisen from the lower classes, but they had all been churchmen. Behind them stood the power of their great corporation. Beyond all his bustling and active movements, Cromwell must have been extremely lonely.

His background is known quite precisely, but not his date of birth. The most likely suggestion is 1485 which would make him just over five years senior to his sovereign. He had been for fifteen years in Wolsey's intimate service, ever since he had been appointed in 1514 as collector of the revenues of the archbishopric of York. He was by that time a lawyer and also in business as a cloth-dresser. A fulling-mill by the waterside at Putney had been in his family's hands for half a century. There was also some land at Wimbledon. Like Sir William Cecil a generation later, he took pleasure in the fresh country air of the Common there. He was also, an occupation which grew with the years, a moneylender. He came from the middle ranks of urban life; he had nothing in common with the few capitalists of the great city companies.

His family life can be described with some exactness. His wife, about whom nothing is known to us, was Elizabeth widow of Thomas Williams and daughter of Henry Wykes of Putney, shearman. She died at Stepney in 1527 before Cromwell appeared upon the stage of history. He never took another wife, but for some years his mother-in-law Mrs Pryor lived in his house[1] as did her second husband. He had two sisters, Catherine who married Morgan Williams an ale brewer and inn keeper at Putney, from whom Oliver Cromwell would descend, and Elizabeth the wife of Mr Wellyfed. His own children and his sisters' children made up his family. He had no adult to help him on his way.

It is curious that, with the exception of a single wealthy stock, he never made any marriages for his humble family. At the beginning he had very much the moneylender's point of vantage, that is to say he had intimate contacts with the aristocracy only upon a single subject. It was his understanding of money that would prove the golden key to gain the King. For the rest he had a very pleasant manner, easy and smooth and most emollient. It was this last quality perhaps which led women easily to put their trust in him. It became evident as the years went on that he had more success with the abbesses than with the abbots.

The service of the Cardinal of York had perhaps inevitably given an ecclesiastical note to his adventures. Thus his second visit to Italy in the reign of Pope Julius II was undertaken to obtain indulgences and other privileges for the guild of Our Lady attached to St Botolph's church at Boston. It seems certain that at an earlier date he had served as a foot soldier in Italy and he had got to know the works of Machiavelli. In his later life he told Archbishop Cranmer 'what a ruffian he had been in his young days'.

Cromwell had been in Parliament since 1523 and now sat for Taunton. He had served the Cardinal in the suppression of the small monasteries whose land had been required to set up his new colleges at Oxford and at Ipswich. Wolsey had received authority for this action from the Holy See. Cromwell followed the accustomed practices. Thus his will made in 1529 contained the normal

---

[1] These names are found in the inventory dated 26 June 1527 and printed in *Letters and Papers*, pp. 1454-7.

provision[1] for Masses to be said for his soul by the five Orders of Friars with houses in the capital. The Cardinal, perhaps, never took him very seriously; but Cromwell realized quite clearly that what the Cardinal could do, he might do too.

His mind was bent upon his golden talisman, the manipulation of money for the royal service. His early experience had foreshadowed all that might be obtained by a liquidation of the monasteries or to put it in the way it must have come to him by the liquidation of monastic holdings. It was not in any easy-going King to resist the offer that he made to him. This went side by side with a solution to the Spanish marriage crisis; but theology was not the interest of Thomas Cromwell. His concern was all contained within the kingdoms of this world.

With this there went his great power as an organizer and the work that fell to him almost unconsciously as the creator of a civil service. Once the papal tie was broken, the Crown remained as the paymaster and the sole rewarder of all its servants. It is not clear how far he was really conscious of this great work that he would do; but it is worth noting that in his lonely life Cromwell alone had an equal contact with those who can be best described as the embryonic members of a civil service, men in fact like Roland Lee, who ruled Wales and reorganized the Marches.

It is natural that he should greatly value the work of Machiavelli. He knew that he could only do his work on behalf of the Prince and with his mandate. Cromwell had a very precise knowledge of money values, somewhat rare in that period. By the time that he was forty he had understood what each man might require of him. It was knowledge of a kind that would be useful in the eighteenth century, in fact for so long as the Prince survived. It is not unreasonable to see him as the first of a line of English statesmen, which reached its apogee with Robert Walpole. Upon the other side there are resemblances to the work carried through against the Church in Portugal by the Marquis de Pombal. He had that leader's cold embracing vision. It is an irony that what Pombal did for the King of Portugal, the *Rex Fidelissimus*, Cromwell carried forward for the Defender of the Faith. He was truly

[1] Will of Thomas Cromwell of London, dated 12 July 1525, *Letters and Papers*, pp. 2573 ff.

anxious to have as little trouble as might be in sweeping away the monastic system and in liberating for the royal disposal the many square miles of monastic land.

One gains a curious impression of his house in London, against the gate of the Austin Friars in 1527. It shows Cromwell at the beginning of his high career. If the contents of the house suggests something of the magpie, Cromwell was still the servant. He had not come yet to his great estate. One is first struck by the chests.[1] In the room adjoining the new chamber there was a great ship chest, bound with flat bars of iron of Flanders work, all covered with yellow leather. In the private chamber next to the hall there was a great round ship chest. There were also two others, one in the leaden house and one in the old parlour. There were also various fixings belonging to his master, His Grace's arms in gilt on canvas in the hall and in the parlour my Lord Cardinal's arms painted and gilt.

In the parlour there was also a great glass in the window. There were painted tables of Our Lord and of Our Lady and of Lucrezia Romana. In one of the servants' chambers there were two images in gilt leather of Our Lady and St Christopher and a *mappa mundi* of paper, lined with canvas. Somewhere about the house there was another *mappa mundi*, stained. Under the stairs there was an image of St Anthony in golden leather.

In the new chamber there was a carved and gilded altar with a picture of Our Lord's Nativity. There was a great double gilt salt with a cover and images, and a smaller gilt salt and a little bottle of rose water. The objects are recounted in a pell-mell fashion. There was a table set with the King's arms and an image of Carolus the Emperor. In the parlour and the hall there were six cushions of verdure, the latter set wrought with the red rose and the pomegranate. There were a variety of beds and a couple of sets of Dornyx hangings.

The kitchen was well-appointed. In addition to the usual gear there were seven tall candlesticks and a container for marchpane, three little candlesticks set in wooden stocks, an iron toasting fork. There was also in readiness a fine damask tablecloth with curious

---

[1] Inventory dated 26 June 1527, *Letters and Papers*, pp. 1454-7.

flowers and a diaper tablecloth that was sewn with a pattern of crossed diamonds.

Master Cromwell's own clothing was of good quality. A carved and gilded wainscot press contained a gown furred with budge and another with black damask, and beside them an old night gown faced with fox. There was a riding coat of brown and blue, welted with tawny velvet, an old russet gown lined with black lamb and numerous doublets. These were all of satin, five black, two crimson and one russet. There was a fine black gown embroidered with martins; a sword of Marion's making, gilded and with a black velvet scabbard; a black satin hat; a riding cape; twelve pairs of gloves.

The jewellery was at this date extensive. There were eleven rings; including a diamond, a rock ruby, an amethyst, a jacynth and a turquoise. All these were set in gold. There was a golden *Agnus Dei* with an engraving of Our Lady and St George. There were eight pearls on a string; a diamond rose. This was an inventory taken at a date of no importance. It reveals in a very natural fashion Master Cromwell as he made his way.

He was the ablest man about the ageing Cardinal when disaster overtook him. There is a certain dispute as to his action at this time; but he probably did all within reason that he could to aid the falling statesman. No man and least of all the Cardinal would have expected him to go down in that shipwreck. He had aided Wolsey with his advice and had apparently suggested to him that he should convey some lands of the see of Winchester to Mistress Boleyn and her young brother. It can hardly be said that Cromwell would look with favour on the young Boleyns; they were too distant from his ranging mind. It was in no sense a betrayal that he would in time contrive to bring them down.

The Cardinal went up to York to visit for the first time his own archbishopric. It was here that his fortunes began to founder. In a sense he had too much protection; he was too well armoured. His situation resembled that of the Cardinal of Brandenburg. All the circumstances of his life had built up his position. He was a man who was made for manoeuvres; but there was no opportunity for him to manoeuvre if his master should decide to quarrel with the Holy See.

The idea that the Cardinal might have lived quietly in his arch-diocese of York was indeed a mirage. Where indeed could a cardinal live in those hard times? It is rather curious that the King should have been so slow in getting rid of him. The sovereign was of course still a youngish man and his whims had not yet come to stamp out his gratitude. At the same time it must have been clear that there could be no return unless the King gave up his proposed marriage. It appears that there was very little feeling in Rome for the Cardinal of England; his Hat had been won from the former pontiff by the King's wishes. As in the fifteenth century, the Vatican did not give much thought to the miseries of foreign members of the Sacred College. The case of Louis IX and Cardinal Balue is one example. It was recognized that in a measure the King of France had the right to deal as he thought fit with the Cardinal of Angers when the sphere involved was wholly political.

It is often at the moment of catastrophe that we can see in exact detail a man's possessions. And this comes out the more clearly in Wolsey's case for he was the last of his great line. In the stable of the northern primate at Cawood Castle there were still those beasts which would never be seen again upon the roads of England, the cross horse, a great grizzled gelding with all his harness, and the pillar horse, a black trotting horse called Metcalf with his apparel of broad leather. This was the end of all the Legatine insignia. There was also the Cardinal's own saddle for a white dappled grey hoby with black velvet apparel. There was likewise a grey and white ambling mule with his own fittings of black velvet.[1]

In the chapel at Cawood, besides a pair of altar candlesticks of gilt plate, there was a set of red cloth vestments for a priest, deacon and subdeacon, made after the Roman fashion.[2] The tapestries in his northern home were few, after all he had never been there. One set dealt with the adventures of the Prodigal Son and there was Job sitting on his dunghill and also the story of Celydonia. There were sixteen hangings of tapestry and verdours and fourteen silk cushions.

In York Place in London there was rather more. The chapel

---

[1] *Letters and Papers*, vol. IV, part III, 1529–30, p. 3045.
[2] *ibid.*, p. 3045.

12 Sir Thomas Elyot

13 Sir Henry Guldeford

14 William Reskimer

15 Sir John Godsalve

plate there included[1] a monstrance for the sacrament to be borne
in procession, a deep goblet and a standing cup, the latter a present
from the Abbot of Abingdon. They had both covers set with saints,
the first St Dunstan and the second St George. These were, perhaps, *ciboria*. It is at York Place that we first come on jewellery, a
bowl of gold with a cover garnished with diamonds, rubies, pearls
and sapphires, and a set of six gold spoons, a gold strawer for
oranges. Still these represented just the last months of his life. The
real background of the Cardinal's magnificence was Hampton
Court.

In the great mass of hangings,[2] it is rather curious how many
scenes were drawn from the Old Testament. Thus there were
pieces dealing with the history of Absalom and Samson and that
of King Assueres and Queen Esther. There were histories of Jacob
and Susanna and 'Holyfernes'; eight pieces dealt with Salamon.
The hangings with religious themes were more expected; the new
rich Arras on a red ground, lined with buckram, of the Passion of
Christ, Our Lady and her Son, the tokens of the Passion, the five
joys of Our Lady and her Assumption. There was an offering of a
cluster of grapes in a cup, Veronica holding a vernacle, the Salutation. There was a tapestry of Christ bearing His Cross and the
Jews all crying *Crucifige*. There were pictures of St Ambrose and
St Gregory and St Jerome; but then we enter a more unknown
field. There was a portrait of the Emperor Trajan and then of
Dame Pleasaunce. There was one which is called the Duke of Bry.
Was this perhaps some memory of the work of the Duke of Berri?
Another is simply called the 'gyaunte Orrible'. There was a
tapestry dealing with King Charles, a name impossible to decypher,
and the old hangings of the hall at Westminster with gryphes and
gryphons and the words *memento*.

In some cases their provenance is given. Quite a few had come
from the executors of Bishop Ruthall, who had held the see of
Durham, and four from the late Bishop of London. These were a
set superscribed with the words *O pie, o clemens, o dulcis Maria*.
Others had representations of Judas, and a ship and David harp-
ing. There was always a regular supply from Richard Gresham,
master of the Mercers' Company. It was these last which probably

---

[1] *ibid.*, p. 2771.   [2] *ibid.*, pp. 2763–70.

came direct from the Low Countries. There were many sets and some were old and worn.

This is just a selection. There was also some of the *impedimenta* which the Cardinal had taken to Guines to the Field of the Cloth of Gold. And then there was the jewellery, a ruby ring wherewith the King was sacred, 234 other rings, five small ropes of pearls and 104 pearls lying loose. There were 454 buttons of roses.

There were the chairs of estate of cloth of tissue and cloth of gold, the many carpets for all the window ledges, the great chairs bearing a cardinal's hat and a double cross each worked in Venice gold on crimson satin. There was a bedstead of alabaster with the Lord Legate's arms and gilded flowers. On a cushion of green and blue velvet there lay the Cardinal's Mass book.

These are all here set out for they represented that old world which would vanish as soon as the cardinalate should cease to be a preoccupation of the English State. One feels that perhaps Cromwell alone realized quite clearly the nature of the change that was upon them. The Cardinal was boxed up at York where there could be no future for him. Once he was in the north the pressures against him mounted quickly. He was arrested by the King's command and brought south towards the capital. He died at Leicester Abbey on his journey through that rainy autumn on 4 November 1530 and was buried there. The next year Catherine was removed to the Moor, his home, in Hertfordshire. On 1 September 1532 Anne Boleyn was created Marchioness of Pembroke. Her private marriage took place about 25 January following and this was officially announced by the King at Easter. The second section of the great reign had begun.

Archbishop Warham was now dead. The King had got to fill the two archbishoprics. The choice for Canterbury was not long delayed, but was in fact quite unexpected. The Emperor's Court had travelled down into Lombardy when the summer heats were over and they were clustered in the little town of Mantua when a messenger from England reached the English Ambassador, the Archdeacon of Taunton. He was to return home and accept the nomination to the primatial see. Dr Cranmer was a small lithe figure, a good horseman from an obscure stock of gentle blood, a product of Cambridge and devoted to his master and sovereign.

He had been bound up for some years with the Boleyn effort to free the King from his first marriage. For the purpose the choice could not have been improved upon for he was not only a Regalian, but was a true and exact Protestant in the sense of the Protest of Speyer. The only part of Europe that he really knew was Germany and there the Roman cause was crumbling. He had a sense of literary cadences and his character was mild and timorous. Except for the Anabaptists to whom no one showed mercy, he had a certain tendency to be merciful. He was too Regalian, it seems, to understand how any man could hold out against the King's known wishes and expressed desires. The early Lutherans had this same entwinement.

Cranmer was not extravagant and not luxurious. He lived with some modesty at Lambeth Palace. How did he survive throughout the reign with such success? The answer may be that he never sought to penetrate the veil which hid the majesty of his great sovereign. He had been married as a young man in Cambridge before he took Orders and as a widower he had made a second marriage in Germany before his nomination to the primacy; this he kept secret. It seems that until almost the end of his life he was happy. Among the early Protestants, the Lutheran world especially had always tended to praise the State. God would choose different sovereigns as instruments to strike down the papal monarchy.

Therefore no one was more willing than Archbishop Cranmer to undertake the solution of the King's marriage problems in the Pope's despite. All that Henry might do to remove the papal top-hamper from the English scene received his warm support. At the same time he had a reverential attitude towards the King's theology. As far as the Court life was concerned he hardly counted. From the point of view of Thomas Cromwell he had great assets. He was unfalteringly loyal to their master's will and he was without links with those Court factions who were necessarily opposed to each new minister. It must have been very easy for Cromwell to talk to him in the quiet of Lambeth and to assess those views which his gentle character held to with such tenacity. As an ally, therefore, he had almost every advantage. In fact he had them all save one and that was courage.

It was in these years that the high posts came to Thomas Cromwell. It became evident very early that he and he alone could perform great services to the Crown and particularly in the matter of obtaining the transfer of all monastic properties to the civil power. Since no one else could do what he would do, there was no open opposition to the posts which came to him from other courtiers. Early in 1531 he had been created a privy councillor and in the following year he received the mastership of the Jewel House. This would be a convenient position when the jewels which had been laid up among the church gear and in the shrines became dispersed. In the next year he became Chancellor of the Exchequer, then a relatively unimportant post, and Recorder of Bristol. He held both these until his death. In April 1534 he reached the key position of principal secretary to the King. In the next year he received the office, also a life appointment, as Chancellor, High Steward and Visitor of the University of Cambridge. He was now the man best qualified to do the King a needed service. Still before he could settle down to his great work, there were two problems which had arisen from the King's divorce. They concerned the fate of two high officers, the Bishop of Rochester and Sir Thomas More.

V

The Bishop of Rochester

Alone among the great figures of the reign John Fisher, Bishop of Rochester, stood entirely outside it. He belonged in spirit to an earlier time, to that Cambridge generation which was already in middle life at the beginning of the century. Even then he was in certain ways old-fashioned. It was King Henry VII's mother the Lady Margaret, who had persuaded her son to propose him for the diocese of Rochester as long ago as 1504. He had little in common with those many bishops whose promotion had come to them through the royal service. An impression of Bishop Fisher can be gained by a study of those Holbein drawings from which his tired, farseeing eyes gaze wearily on the great reign and its new splendour.[1] Each reaction to the increasingly complex world by which he was surrounded deserves to emphasize his deep simplicity. The moment of his arrest appears the best point at which to study what was to the world of the Court, an alien figure. At this stage, too, the State Papers provide a view of the domestic interior at Rochester, the minute detail of his poverty, the broken peace.

By the spring of 1534 Henry VIII's divorce case was over, the religious schism quite effective, the breach with Rome almost complete, and the Bishop could gain but little consolation from the Easter festival. On the following 16 April his arrest, as the defender of the ancient discipline, seemed the mere final step, long since foreseen of what was to the Bishop's thought this tragic progress. The movement of men's minds must have appeared to him inscrutable, that rejection and questioning of the verities with which, since childhood, he had been familiar. For just thirty years he had ruled his see, riding on horseback through the Kentish country,

[1] Cf. portrait reproduced facing p. 65.

with a period of preaching or confirming to vary the rhythm of his constant prayer.

The scepticism of the new age, the King with his carnality and self-communings, the sacrilege of heresy bore down on one whose life of prayer had led him far from worldly interests. Religion, in the sense of the practice of the Sacramental life and the absorption of the Testaments which the Church had guarded, alone seemed clear. It was the reality from which the world was moving. Serene amid this indifference the Bishop prayed with the forms which he had used in his distant boyhood as he had knelt by his father's grave beneath the rood in the minster at Beverley. He would always raise his heart to God in the same allegiance. The words of the Easter Sequence *Victimas paschali laudes* came with the memory of the voices of the clerks and the singing men of his cathedral.

This same Faith and the tranquillity bred of an earlier and more peaceful time were alike implicit in every movement of the chaplains and the servants in that great ill-built house, the palace of Rochester. This had been the scene of his austerities and his quiet ruling. The bare untapestried walls of his sleeping chamber, with the green and white embroidered silk behind the altar in the corner and the rough blue sarcenet curtains by the window had that familiarity that would come to a cell loved and well kept. Beside one wall there stood the Bishop's bed with its counterpane of red linen sewed on the underside with canvas, which covered the hard straw matting of his night's discomfort. Each detail of the room bore witness to a struggle for detachment from the things of sense and a determined following of the ancient ways. During thirty years the Bishop had looked out upon the view from these same windows, the flooding and uncovering of the tide banks, the gulls, the empty shore.

About him the worn equipment of the house and its empty spaces suggested that love of the poverty of the Gospels which he followed without the constraint of vow. The study place and the dining chamber both bore his austere impress, the table and the long forms and the Bishop's chair with its black velvet. The grave and careful reading of a clerk moving through the Gregorian homilies would mark a fitting background to the scene, while the

Bishop sat alone in his dark moth-eaten tippet, his wide jaws moving slowly as he munched the bread in his thin pottage.

Upon the bare table stood a skull to keep him company, beyond the mazer bowl and the little silver cellars. Such silver ware, small in quantity and in value, had come, as had so many of his possessions from his patroness the Lady Margaret, the old King's mother. Personal acquisition did not square with his conception of the pastoral role.

When erect, with the hair shirt grating on him constantly, his emaciated figure only added to the impression of unexpected height. In his face the blue veins showed more clearly now that his seventies were far advanced. The spare white-haired figure, with those eyes which marked his detachment from the world so plainly, suggests the last months of some early Bishop in the Christian centuries.

Beneath him in the town the travellers from the Cinque Ports jostled and in the Medway lay the Gravesend wherries. With the casual strangers he had small concern, but the innkeepers and the other townsmen and the close-gathered households of that Kentish country were of his flock. He could not fail to remember that God would hold him as steward for their Faith and his own. Bishop Fisher's thoughts upon this matter, his great sense of the duties of the pastoral offices and of the feeding of the sheep, are presented in the sermon which he preached upon the books of Martin Luther. 'And Peter,' the Bishop had declared,[1] 'was made by Christ, to whom he commysed in his absence the cure of the Christen people sayenge: *pasce oves meas, pasce, pasce.*' One word sums up the Bishop of Rochester in life and death—*pasce, pasce.*

The meaning of his arrest, the steps by which the King had separated from the Holy See, the casting off from the unity of Christian Faith were seen without illusion, events sharply defined and evil. It was not with the Court that his own sympathies had ever lain, nor his career depended. The piety and old-fashioned scholarship, the careful fine calligraphy, the controlled appreciation of good letters, would all seem to have marked out Dr Fisher for a life of learning and quiet pastoral care; the stole, the doctor's

---

[1] Cf. Bishop Fisher, *English Works*, ed. Professor J. E. B. Mayor, 1876.

cap; hardly the mitre. The crucial accident which had uprooted him from his Cambridge life must have come back to him, that choice as confessor to King Henry VII's mother, the Lady Margaret.

It is strange how remote that world must now have seemed, the cameo-like form of the Lady Margaret, the high coif and the folded linen beneath the chin, the mild wide eyes, the figure, prim and diminutive. She would sit with her hands folded before her Book of Hours, while her quiet speech fell on matters of the spirit, as she told of the dream of St Nicholas before her marriage; a miniature from an older time. Hers had been a figure staid and a little aloof, as she arranged her household and her bounties in the purposed chastity of her third espousals.

It was upon these bounties that there had hinged the Bishop's chief administrative labours, the founding of St John's and Christ's Colleges at Cambridge and the Lady Margaret chairs of Divinity. But twenty-five years had passed since the Lady Margaret had died, and customs changed quite quickly. That reading of Hylton and the ghostly counsel, the filagree of her devotion, to Our Lady's Nativity for instance, the whole devout way of living had now vanished down the wind. Yet such a spirit had never been at ease in the Court atmosphere. The new strange world in which the Bishop moved appeared in the light of his detachment with frosted clearness.

Even his relations with Queen Catherine were hardly simple. She was devout in her own Spanish fashion, to Walsingham and the Franciscans; she used with persistent care the Latin Office. Yet it was surely difficult for the Bishop, a Yorkshireman, direct and very humble, to fathom the Queen's reserved mind and its mainsprings, the heavily conscious royalty of the new Spanish kingdom, the barred, yet tremulous, Castilian pride. He was not her confessor and was only consulted upon occasion. It was George de Athequa, the Spaniard whom the King had promoted to the see of Llandaff, who understood her.

The Bishops of the Court party moved in circles, which his own orbit never touched, while day by day their contact with the King enmeshed them in those toils of the royal policy from which his own detached life kept him free. 'Now be many chalices of gold,' the Bishop of Rochester had written,[1] 'but almost no golden priests.' Difficult as it is to indicate his own remoteness, some impression is conveyed by his biographer. 'Truly,' this Marian admirer wrote[2] of Fisher, 'of all the bishops that we have knowne or heard of in our daies, it may best be said, that this bishopp hath well lived and well and truly lurked: for who at any time hath seen him ydle walk or wander.' Through the strange phrasing the special quality of his life comes clear.

As he moved on towards prison the new Court life was present to him, that magnificence, high coloured, rather vulgar, which the late Cardinal Wolsey loved. It must have been an unsavoury remembrance that Master Cromwell had survived from the dead Cardinal's gaudy wreck. The Bishop had no prejudice against new men, for he was one himself, a mercer's son from Beverley; but he could feel the loss of true religion. The politicians shared the courtiers' indifference. One appetite was common to them both, and the Bishop knew to his sorrow the riches of the Church.

The Bishop stood for the old ways and the heart of England. It was clear that he must now defend his flock, as they dug and ploughed and chaffered, faithful and simple. The literary and scholarly friendships of the past had worn thin in this testing time. Erasmus was now remote and his action doubtful. As the Bishop remembered that great scholar, whom he had befriended in Cambridge long ago, their conversations must have seemed so far away. The details of the visits were far back in the memory; the heavy cloak and rich black furs from out of Germany showing dark against the poor wall hangings, as the scholar played with an ivory sand caster or other toy in his quiet talking. No man could be more pleasant to those whom he admired than Erasmus. The young painter from Basel whom he had sent – Hans Holbein, a mere name upon the memory – had spoken of him. But in this stress a certain triviality marked such scenes. The Bishop was absorbed in his single duty to protect, as an *alter Christus*, the flock of Christ.

Behind him lay his own diocese, and the experience of the German Wars had shown the insecurity of religious practice, once the unity of Christian Faith was broken. He knew that he could count on Sir Thomas More's clear conscience, but the strength of the

[1] *ibid.*   [2] *ibid.*

new monarchy, the pervading influence of the Tudor power and
the well-executed manoeuvres of the Court had left them now in
isolation. The King's counsellors were most subtle, as had been
proved in the case of the nun of St Sepulchre's at Canterbury and
her treasonable sayings, in which the Bishop had so nearly been
involved; but all that was required in these last stages was to go
forward in the light of Faith.

In the churches, hospitals and chapels the Holy Sacrifice of the
Mass was offered and the shriving and receiving of the Sacrament
renewed the life of Grace for the Christian people. In his countryside the religious houses stood as firmly rooted as the oak in which
St Simon Stock found refuge; while the pattern of each shrine
would stand out clear. An atmosphere of high spiritual doctrine
marked Dartford, the Bishop's sister's convent, Dominican, a
school for manners and good letters, with its strict well-born community, whose diluted conservatism still showed through their
courteous phrases. The calefactory at Greenwich brought back
another scene: the form of Master Forrest, keen and busy, and the
tough, austere Franciscans; while at Aylesford in its quiet elms the
shadow of St Simon lay upon the Carmelites in their simplicity.
At Boxley, just beyond his border, there stood the abbey of the
Rood of Grace. Here was the ordered religion of the Christian
centuries, now threatened. The light of the spring days fell upon
these houses with the first apple blossom in their orchards in the
calm weather. The Bishop could not forget for an instant that God
had raised him up as their protector. In this lull before the storm
there was no movement. The disturbances of the Court found reflection in the religious peace which lay unbroken on the see of
Rochester. The freshening breeze from off the Channel slowly
turned the sails of windmills.

In another region also, the freshness and the limitations of the
medieval knowledge defined his thought, while the restrained
quality of his imagination kept the whole, as in a miniature, within
due limits. The very restrictions of his knowledge had brought the
Holy Land closer to him than to the later ages. 'The Blessed
Martha,' he had declared[1] in one of his more carefully wrought-
out sermons, 'was a woman of noble blode to whom by inheritaunce

[1] *ibid.*

belonged the castel of Bethany.' The Ancients, too, had come within his ken, and he was still sufficiently medieval in his concepts to realize spontaneously and humbly how closely he approached the sum of knowledge. 'Where is now,' the Bishop had declaimed[1] with his native rhetoric, 'the immemorial company and puyssance of Xerxes and Caesar, where is now the grete victoryes of Alexander and Pompey, where is now the grete rychesse of Cresus and Crassus.'

The intermingling of these strands of thought, the curveting simplicity of the Bishop's pastoral rhetoric, is seen in his sermon on Martin Luther. 'Such a clowde,' he wrote[2] of the early heretics, 'was Arrius which stered so greate a tempest that many years after it vexyd the chirche of Christe. And after hym came many other lyke clowdes as Macedonius, Nestorius, Eutices, Donatus, Ioinianus, Pellagius, Johennes Wicleff with other moor. . . . And nowe suche another clowde is raysed alofte one Martyn Luther a frere, the which has stered a myghty storm and tempeste in the chirche and hath shadowed the clere lyght of many scrytures of God.'

It was on the Thursday after *Dominica in Albis*, in that Eastertide of 1534, that Bishop Fisher was brought down to London to the Tower. Through this week in the liturgical calm of the Paschal Season the Proper of the Mass had remained unchanging. 'And there are three that give testimony on earth', the meaning would come to him as his failing eyes peered towards the missal with the Lady Margaret's portcullis on the cover, 'the spirit and the water and the blood'. How strongly the Epistle would sound forth as a demand and as a warning. *Et tres sunt qui testimonium dant in terra: spiritus et aqua et sanguis.* It was a not unfitting prelude to the leadership of the white-robed army, *te martyrum candidatus.* This was really a different world from that with which the Court was occupied.

As the gates of the Tower of London closed behind him the Bishop had marked his future. The imprisonment lasted for a year and during this time several priests were executed for their refusal to accept the Royal Supremacy; on 4 May 1535 Dom John

---

[1] *ibid.*

[2] *ibid.*, p. 46. For certain details cf. *The Life of Fisher* transcribed from Harleian MS. 1621 by the Rev. Ronald Bayne, E.E.T.S. 1921.

Houghton, Prior of the London Charterhouse and the Carthusian priors of Beauvale and Axholme and Richard Reynolds, a Bridgettine, and three weeks later Dom Humphrey Middlemore, Dom William Exmewe and Dom Sebastian Newdigate, the two former being respectively the vicar and procurator of the London Charterhouse. Finally on 22 June 1535 the Bishop of Rochester was also put to death for his refusal to accept the Royal Supremacy and for his statement that 'the King our sovereign lord is not supreme head on earth of the Church of England'. In the previous month he had received the title of Cardinal Priest of the church of St Vitalis. He died that the English provinces might still remain within the unity of the Catholic Faith.

Naturally it can be said that the Bishop's personal experience was at any rate in great part limited to religious houses which reflected his own fervour. In his mind there was no place for those accommodations which had been the daily bread of the late Cardinal of York. He was far also from the men of the younger generation of those stocks which had once formed the White Rose aristocracy. He had never exercised that flattery which the King as a young theologian would expect from all the world of high ecclesiastics.

Further he alone was unaffected by those tide-rips which played about the Court. Piety at this time was not in fashion. There was something exciting in the new world that was opening up before the courtiers, the unlooked-for chance of gold. This was a matter that the Bishop of Rochester had always disregarded. It was, however, what the cool mind of Master Cromwell had long dwelt upon. It was gold seen in the term of pensions which would be proposed for each abbot or abbess, and above all in that golden opportunity which would come to those who could now gather the riches of the monasteries. One had to remember the halcyon weather which was the background to all that time. No set of courtiers had ever had this opportunity, the miles of monastic England now offered to them. One should never underestimate the land hunger of the rich.

VI

Lord Chancellor More

Sir Thomas More, who was Lord Chancellor under Henry VIII
and was subsequently tried and executed and in the eyes of Catho-
lics suffered martyrdom, was an unique figure among the victims
of the Reformation period. He was the only high officer of state to
be killed in any country for his adherence to the Old Religion. It
was nevertheless not in any way surprising. He did not belong to
the accustomed range of Tudor politicians. In his youth he had
considered the possibility of joining the London Charterhouse and
for many years he was one of the leading controversialists on the
Roman side. He found a gusto in theological arguments which to
the rest of the King's ministers would seem bizarre.

He was well aware of the weaknesses of the Church in his own
day; but he was deeply shocked by Martin Luther's marriage with
Catherine von Bora. He had a profoundly legal approach to all
such questions. He was used to concubinage on the part of an
Augustinian; it was marriage within a legislative framework that
he abhorred. More also had a life-long devotion to the Blessed
Sacrament. So often in his writings one can find an urgent sense of
the growth of Lutheranism on the Continent.

A letter written by More to the University of Oxford is worth re-
printing for what it tells of his field of reference. He had been
speaking against a man who quoted always from the *Sentences*. 'Or
perhaps he thinks that the whole of theology is contained within
the limits of those *Sentences* on which such as he are always disputing, for the knowledge of which I confess that little enough Latin
is wanted. But to confine theology, the august Queen of Heaven,
within such narrow limits would not only be iniquitous but im-
pious. For does not theology also dwell in the Sacred Scriptures,
and did it not thence make its way to the cells of all the ancient

holy Fathers, I mean Augustine, Jerome, Ambrose, Cyprian, Chrysostom, Cyril, Gregory, and others like them, with whom the study of theology made its abode for more than a thousand years after the Passion of Christ.'[1]

This quotation proves how very far he was from the life of a courtier. His great legal career and in particular the lord chancellorship to which he came in time had brought him in contact with the King, but not with the royal entourage. His upbringing in Cardinal Morton's household and his own distinguished legal background would not have brought him into the life of politics save for his office. Thus the scene at Chelsea in More's garden, where the King would manifest his clear good will as he walked up and down with his arm about More's neck was a forecast of the coming chancellorship. And at this period of his life, the King had a sunny nature, when things went well with him.

At the same time More's life was private. That gay and almost riotous domesticity, in an age when a family's intercourse seemed sometimes frozen, had little contact with the royal palace or the Court. The oak presses and the long tables of his house at Chelsea, the green sward by the river, the scent still hanging in the hayfields defined his setting. He had established himself modestly in the twenty acres of meadow land and planted alleys that he had bought. In the evening when the Law Courts had risen he would return to his family waiting here in the house and gardens, where the river slipped past beneath the terrace which linked the New Building with his barns. Out in the fairway at his back the eight watermen, resting on their oars, kept in readiness the Chancellor's barge which had just brought him from the stairs at Westminster.

In every action a heartening sense of reality appeared through all his gaiety. Henry Patenson, his private fool, would represent one facet and the collections of his animals, the ape and the weasel 'and such beasts as were rare and not common'[2] in their turn marked his quiet hilarity. As a young man especially he was full of fun. This is reflected in a poem[3] which he published in 1516;

---

[1] *Correspondence of Sir Thomas More*, ed. E. F. Rogers (1947), 60.

[2] Nicholas Harpsfield, *Life of More*, Early English Text Society, 1932, 143.

[3] Four lines run, 'With many a sadde stroke, They roll and rumble, They turne and tumble, As pygges do in a poke.' This is printed with a commentary by E. F. Reynolds in *The Field is Won* (1968), 46–7.

it appears to have been made some thirteen years earlier for a feast at Lambeth Palace.

As Sir Thomas sat at his board drinking[1] the small ale of his preference, while he digested the coarse well-leavened bread and the salt meats, the tide of his family flowed about him, amid the speech of the new arts from Italy. And each movement was lit by his calm humour, while through all he had a consciousness of God's protection. 'Whosoever will marke', he had once said,[2] 'the devil and his temptations shall finde him therein much like as an ape, not well looked unto will be busie and bolde to doe shrewde turnes.' Beneath the table played his wife's chained monkey.

An episode in the Harpsfield life records his passing relationship with the Duke of Norfolk. 'He used, being Chancellor[3] to sit and sing in the choir with a surplice on his back. And when the Duke of Norffolks coming at a tyme to Chelsey to dyne with him fortuned to find him in his attire and trace going homewards after servyce, arme in arme with him, said after this fashion: "God body, God body, my Lord Chancellour, a parishe clarke, a parishe clarke. You dishonour the King and his office." ' The Duke of Norfolk was not a man to fail to keep appropriate contacts. It must have been soon plain to him that Sir Thomas More had little contact with those lines of thought that moved the springs of government.

As a young man More had been influenced by Pico della Mirandola and had written his *Life of Johan Picus* printed in 1511. Behind all his ideas lay his long and intimate friendship with Erasmus. There is also one constant factor in More's outlook, his own deep Royalism. This is worth a more than cursory examination, for it is one of the central factors of Tudor England. More came from a legal family established in London. His father Sir John More was a judge and he was by patrimony a freeman of the Mercers' Company. His feeling for the Crown was second nature to him. It is shown in the expressions that More was accustomed to use in speaking of his sovereign. 'I had always used myself,' he wrote to his daughter Margaret, 'to looking first upon God and next upon the King, according to the lesson his Highness taught me at my

---

[1] Description printed in Harpsfield, *op. cit.*, 141–3.
[2] *ibid.*, 77.   [3] *ibid.*, p. 64.

first coming to his noble service.' The same phrase is repeated quite exactly 'which most gracious words was the first lesson also that ever his Grace gave me at my first coming into his noble service'. These were both private letters and therefore deserve more weight than the epitaph that Sir Thomas More composed for his own tomb. This refers to 'the incomparable kindness of his most indulgent King'.[1]

He had, of course, received the kindness of his young sovereign. But that was the King when his sap was running. In those days he was always kind to servants who would give him respect well mixed with admiration. What did he really feel about Sir Thomas More? There was More's circle of scholars, now mostly dead, like Colet and Grocyn. Henry may not have been at ease with all this wisdom. Still there is clearly one thing he wanted. As his marriage case wound on the King became anxious that his learned Chancellor should support the sober conclusions of his royal master.

This problem fell, as did so much within these years, to a great extent on the King's new secretary, Cromwell. It was a different matter from that presented by old Bishop Fisher. In Fisher's case there was no warmth of feeling on the King's part and there were advantages in making an example of an old-fashioned member of the episcopate. It was of great importance to keep the bishops well in line with whatever should prove to be the King's new policy. As far as the episcopate was concerned there would in future be no difficulty. The Lord Chancellor was very different. He had an European reputation and his support was of importance to his own sovereign.

Thomas Cromwell was in a good position to assess both the Lord Chancellor's own learning and the civic position of his family. In his latest book Mr E. F. Reynolds well brings out the efforts that Cromwell made to bring contentment to his master. There was a period of just on two years between Sir Thomas More's resignation of the lord chancellorship in May 1532 and his arrest, and then fifteen months in the Tower of London waited on by his own servant; but More would not accept the breach with Rome nor the justice of the King's second marriage.

Two passages that he wrote in prison help us to form an im-

[1] Reynolds, *op. cit.*, 128, 228 and 259.

16 Anne Boleyn

17 Thomas Boleyn (Earl of Wiltshire), Anne's father

18 William Fitzwilliam,
Earl of Southampton

19 William Fitzwilliam,
Earl of Southampton

pression of More's outlook. One indicates that as he approached the scaffold he had passed beyond that atmosphere of controversy in which so much of his spare time had been involved. He looked forward with hope to a re-integration of Christian doctrine. His thought was very naturally still cast within a late medieval mould; the defence of Christendom against the Moslem East. This passage from *The Dialogue of Comfort* comes in the course of a discussion on the grounds for hope. 'The third,' he wrote,[1] 'is that all Germany, for all their diverse opinions, yet as they agree together in profession of Christ's name, so agree they now together in preparation of a common power in defence of Christendom against our common enemy the Turk. And I trust in God that this shall not only help us to strengthen this war, but also that as God hath caused them to agree together in defence of His name so shall He graciously bring them together in the truth of His faith. Therefore will I let God work and leave off contention; and nothing shall I now say, but that with which they that are themselves of the contrary mind shall have no reason to be discontented.' His long sentences need close attention and are sometimes rather difficult to read. Still, there seems here a form of *clairvoyance* in which Sir Thomas More appears to look forward down the harsh centuries towards the end of controversies.

The next passage also requires a careful reading for it gives More's ultimate judgement which he shared with so few. There is in these words no trace of his Erasmian past. His inner thought goes farther back to the years that he passed with the Carthusians. At the same time his expressions are cast within a framework which is strange to us and perhaps repellent, for he came from a generation which regarded the kingdoms of this world as quite immutable. It is something that he shares from another angle with those writers of the Counter-Reformation, who seem for the same reason quite divorced from the modern spirit. On the other hand there seems in his words a living actuality in his belief in the Catholic doctrine of the Blessed Sacrament. This was something which he shared with the Carthusian martyrs whose life had been passed in silence untouched by the world. They were men withdrawn from the pulsating life around them and the words of the

---

[1] Cf. Reynolds, *op. cit.*, p. 277.

I

Prior of the London Charterhouse, *Moriamur in simplicitate nostra,* let us die in our simplicity, suggest a quality that More alone shared with them, a profound detachment.

It is this character, which some would call sanctity, that separated More from the great Conservative churchmen like Bishop Tunstall and Bishop Gardiner. Such men and their clergy, and the vast flocks dependent on them went very peacefully into a schism which had come upon them. It was none of their devising. The reasons which brought about the Pilgrimage of Grace will be discussed later; but among the courtiers and the great mass of men in the southern shires there was no temptation to disturb the King's Peace.

One has the sense that More's position was not clearly understood by his own family and particularly by his wife and by his sons-in-law, who had their seats in Parliament. One of his writings in the Tower entitled *A Treatise to receive the Blessed Body of our Lord sacramentally and virtually both* gives us an impression of Sir Thomas More at prayer. 'For,' he begins,[1] 'if we will but consider, if there were a great worldly prince which for special favour that he bare us would come visit us in our house, what a business we would then make, and what a work it would be for us, to see that our house were trimmed up in every point, to the best of our possible power, and everything so provided and ordered, that he should [perceive] by his honourable receiving what affection we bear him and in what high estimation we have him. We should soon by the comparing of that worldly prince and his heavenly prince together (between which twain is far less comparison than is between a man and a mouse) inform and teach ourself with how lowly mind, how tender loving heart, how reverent humble manner we should endeavour ourself to receive this glorious heavenly king, the king of all kings, almighty God himself, that so lovingly doth vouchsafe to enter, not only into our house (to which the noble man Centurio acknowledged himself unworthy) but his precious body into our vile wretched carcase, and his holy spirit into our poor simple soul.'

[1] Cf. *ibid.*, pp. 353-4.

VII

Cromwell at Peace

From one angle the fall of Queen Anne may seem fortuitous. There was nothing in the King's policy to endanger her and in the January that followed the execution of Sir Thomas More and Bishop Fisher, Queen Catherine had died. The death of the Dowager Princess of Wales, as she was now styled, would normally have strengthened Queen Anne's position. But in reality her situation was very solitary; she had no one to rely upon save her new husband. It was not within her power to conciliate the King's great officers.

Disappointing as her reign had been to him, her fall could not have failed to exacerbate the Duke of Norfolk. There was always an element of hazard for the man who should obey the King and bring her down. The Duke's manner was always soft and cheerful towards Cromwell for during seven years he controlled the distribution of monastic land to all the courtiers. There came a time when the flow of gold must stop; then the Duke struck. And with the Duke there was another enemy. Dr Stephen Gardiner was a Gallican in the English expression of that term; but like his French counterparts he was before all else an ecclesiastic. There would never be peace with Thomas Cromwell. As far as he was concerned, there was always an east wind in the palace at Winchester. And it was Cromwell's difficulty that both the Duke and the Bishop had a loyalty to the Crown which none could tarnish.

There were only two among his varied ministers whom King Henry used to arrange his intimate concerns and disentangle them, the great Cardinal and Thomas Cromwell. In Cromwell's case the evidence is less clear and it turns really on the question of his responsibility for bringing the charges against Anne Boleyn. In the fall of the two who were closer to him than his other victims, Anne Boleyn and at a later date Thomas Cromwell, the King does not seem to have been responsible in any detail for the charges brought against them. In both cases he accepted a case that other men had constructed for him.

In the case of Queen Anne there seems to be a general agreement as to the falsity of the charges brought against her; but the problem remains as to who was responsible for their construction. In the nature of the case there is no remaining evidence on such a point, but it appears at least most likely that the responsibility rests with Thomas Cromwell.

The King had reached a point at which he was anxious to disembarrass himself of his second Queen. Her failure to bear a son was crucial, but there were also other matters. She had occasional outbursts of temper such as her sovereign never had to bear from his other subjects. The King had become suspicious of her and it is only fair to say that his mind ran on poisoning and on adultery. The Queen was addicted to those mannerisms which life at the Court of France had taught her. She and her few favourite courtiers had a familiarity with the French language and the Gallic customs, which Henry did not share with them.

As she moved forward through the spring and early summer of 1536 she must have been terribly lonely. Her isolation in some ways resembled that of Messalina long ago. Both followed their own courses far removed from their once doting husbands. Queen Catherine's death had been no help to her. The great ladies of the Court had stood around Queen Anne at her coronation; they would not help her now.

The Duke of Norfolk had not liked her patronage of Lutherans; he now drew off from her. Her own father, the Earl of Wiltshire, had the sense to realize that it would be prudent at this time to cut adrift. The Queen was naturally nervous. We can imagine her slender and tall, her hanging sleeves concealing the deformed finger of her left hand as she walked with her Breton greyhound Urian beside her, speaking to the gentlemen about her in that beautiful and modulated voice which in the past the King had loved.

Henry VIII had now decided that Jane Seymour would make a

quiet bride for him. He left the Court at Greenwich and left others
to bring a set of charges against Anne Boleyn. By these her immediate affinity was swept away. She was accused of incest with her
brother George Lord Rochford and of adultery with the members
of her circle, Sir Francis Weston, Henry Norris and William
Brereton, gentlemen of her privy chamber, and Mark Smeeton,
her musician. All except Mark Smeeton denied the charges. Sir
Francis was the son and heir of Sir Richard Weston, who had built
the great house at Sutton Place near Guildford on land which had
been sequestrated from the Duke of Buckingham. The Queen and
her restricted circle all suffered execution. Someone had thought
this out. It seems likely it was Thomas Cromwell.

It would appear that Archbishop Cranmer had little contact
with all this question, although he had been brought in to consider
the matter of Queen Anne's pre-contract. He sat quiet at Lambeth
with his scholarly concerns, looking on with native sympathy
while the old Church of Rome came crumbling down. In May
Anne Boleyn was buried and in July Cromwell was created Lord
Privy Seal. This was the title by which henceforward he was
generally known. In the same month he became Vicar and Vicegerent of the King in Spirituals. He had thus obtained his power;
it remained for him to carry out the work assigned to him.

Crown patronage lay before him like an open field; but it was
his difficulty that he could offer employment to his dependents not
gain his equals. The embryonic civil service formed before his
eyes. The old churchmen as such were now irrelevant in the field
of politics. He would now shape the royal servants to their rôle in
the great kingdom. He looked out upon a world whose management was now becoming in essence wholly secular.

VIII

The Northern Earls

The North of England does not seem to have entered greatly into King Henry's calculations. He had entrusted it to the guardianship of his young son the Duke of Richmond, who had died of consumption in July of this year 1536. Cawood, the residence of the Archbishops of York, had seen the last few months of Cardinal Wolsey's life in 1530. In some ways the Pilgrimage of Grace came out of a clear sky. It was not a quarter from which the King or his Court expected trouble.

There are several surprising factors about the Pilgrimage of Grace. It broke out in a period of comparative calm in the King's affairs. Queen Catherine had died in January and Anne Boleyn had been executed in May. Henry was in the early stages of his quiet marriage to Jane Seymour when the stirs began in the northern counties. At the same time there were two elements in Lincolnshire and Yorkshire which made for instability. The much less important factor was the long standing disaffection of two peers, Lord Darcy and Lord Hussey. They appear to have been in no way associated with the beginning of the Pilgrimage and Robert Aske, its leader, later stated that he had never met Lord Darcy until the rebellion was under way. Lord Darcy had also been recognized for some years by the Government as being disaffected and had been kept in London since 1529. He was now sixty-eight years of age, a soldier of an earlier period. Since the siege of Therouanne in 1513 he had suffered from the stone. He had only recently returned to his home at Templehurst in Yorkshire.

The other and more serious matter was the future of the great Percy properties, the most extensive in the North of England. The fifth Earl, the Duke of Buckingham's brother-in-law, died in 1527 and the whole of this great alliance, with its very many dependent families, had been since then in the feeble hands of his delicate son. The new Earl suffered constantly from ague; his marriage to Lady Mary Talbot, the Earl of Shrewsbury's child, had now broken down and he lived in retirement at Wressell Castle, an old-fashioned stronghold on the drowned water meadows of the Derwent in Howdenshire. This was on the southern edge of his estates. In February 1535 he wrote to Cromwell that on account of 'the debylyty and unnaturalness of his heirs' he had determined to bequeath all his property to the King. This was probably what brought his two next brothers Sir Thomas and Sir Ingram Percy into rebellion. The character and situation of the childless Earl seemed to the Government a heaven-sent opportunity for breaking up this great still semi-feudal entity.

Men had a sort of foreshortened folk memory in the North Country. They had a contempt for Northumberland's poor physique; respect was concentrated on his active brothers. And then of course they did not know the King for he had never come north on progresses. It was this ignorance that led men into the Pilgrimage of Grace.

The present Earl, Sir Henry Percy, spent his youth in Cardinal Wolsey's household. He had been a friend of young Anne Boleyn. And this familiarity with the sovereign was something which the other holders of the northern earldoms shared. Lord Derby was twenty-six. He lived away to the west beyond the area of the rebellion. He had married the Duke of Norfolk's young stepsister. Lord Westmorland was a little older, but he had been endangered once before. His wife was Lady Catherine Stafford and his marriage had taken place before disaster overtook his father-in-law, the Duke of Buckingham. Lord Cumberland was married to Northumberland's elder sister. The Nevilles of Westmreland were growing poorer, while the Cliffords of Cumberland were getting richer. Alone of these four families, the Cliffords had connections both with the world of fashion and with the Court. Cumberland had lately built the Conduit Court at Skipton in Craven; he had introduced early sixteenth-century Flemish hangings into his gallery. He was also arranging an alliance between his eldest son and the Duke of Suffolk's daughter, the King's niece. Henry had granted him his earldom in 1525. One thing these four lords would never do, they would never join the Pilgrimage of Grace.

This rebellion was in two sections and the first had little contact with either the courtiers or the Court. It took place in the scattered parishes in the northern section of Lindsey in Lincolnshire, the wild lands that lay beyond the wolds. The occasion for action was the arrival of the royal commissioners in June to suppress the smaller monasteries and members of these houses, some of the monks from the greater monasteries and a heavy number of the parish priests seem to have joined together to resist them. They were supported by the principal yeomen and also, more strangely, by the smaller squires. In the first flurry of the disorders the Bishop of Lincoln's chancellor Dr Heneage was killed. Nicholas Melton, a shoemaker of Louth, known as Captain Cobbler, and to a lesser extent Matthew Mackerell, the Abbot of Barlings, appear as leaders. The attitude of the various local landowners now seems confused. There were cries against Cromwell and the demand for the removal from the King's Council of the men of villein blood. They were a rabble, not trained to fight and quite unwarlike and they found themselves in danger through the murder of Heneage.

There was one almost accidental victim. Lord Hussey of Sleaford had land in this neighbourhood. He has been seen earlier with Lord Darcy in his negotiations with Lord Monteagle. He was to some extent a self-made man, an old official. He had been sent on various diplomatic missions and had been raised to the peerage as recently as 1529. It seems that he was influenced by his wife Lady Anne Grey a daughter of George Earl of Kent, the head of a very ancient and impoverished stock. She was a noisy supporter of Queen Catherine's daughter the Princess Mary. Hussey was careful and maintained a correspondence with Thomas Cromwell; but while he had not joined, neither had he acted against the rebels in Lincolnshire. He was suspect as Lord Darcy also was suspect. He was among those later executed.

This part of the rebellion might have occurred at any time of lawlessness and Lord Hussey died like any other subject who corresponded with a Foreign Power; but the Yorkshire element in the Pilgrimage was both much more considerable and also more explicable. It was to a great extent an upsurge of the fifteenth century.

The leader, and in fact almost the creator, of the Pilgrimage of Grace was Robert Aske, the one really interesting figure thrown up among these northern rebels. He was a younger son of one of the lesser squires of the lands north of the Humber, born and brought up at his father's house at Aughton in Howdenshire. He had connections among the northern gentry and was a second cousin of Lord Cumberland's; he was a barrister and had been a member of young Northumberland's household, his cousin's brother-in-law. He was compact, energetic and self-confident; he had lost an eye in an accident as a boy. He had the direct outlook of the North Country. The problem is how he could have thought that he might have been successful. I can only suppose that he did not understand the King. In the early part of the reign few men who were not members of the Court itself could grasp at all the character that was developing beneath his heartiness and his royal good will.

Aske was responsible for the proclamation which still makes its appeal to all who understand the ancient ways. With this there was devised 'The Oath of the Honourable Men', which ran as follows.[1] 'Ye shall not enter into this our Pilgrimage of Grace for the Commonwealth, but only for the love that ye do bear unto Almighty God his faith, and to Holy Church militant and the maintenance thereof, to the preservation of the King's person and his issue, to the purifying of the nobility, and to expulse all villein blood and evil councillors against the Commonwealth from his Grace and his Privy Council of the same.'

These were the words of a past century, those hot crusading sentences. One can understand the use of the parish churches, the fires lit on the church towers, not only on the Lincoln side of Humber, but beyond the estuary in Howdenshire. Here at least there was from the beginning the leadership of Sir Ingram and Sir Thomas Percy and the support in that same world from Robert Constable. It was an old-fashioned but an established practice for gentlemen to ride behind a Percy. There was an unity in the North Country which had no replica in the South of England.

Of course it was in part the amount of time that old Northumberland and his younger sons had passed in the North of England that

[1] Cf. Madeleine Hope Dodds and Ruth Dodds, *The Pilgrimage of Grace 1536–1537 and the Exeter Conspiracy 1538* (1915), vol. I, p. 182.

gave them authority in the northern parts. Unlike the other leading family the Nevilles, the Percies had played a canny part in the
civil wars of the last century. Henry Algernon fifth Earl of Northumberland appears to have been known as the Magnificent. He
was the head of his family from 1489 until 1527 and had been
made a Knight of the Garter in 1495 when he was seventeen. Like
his son after him, he lived in the southern parts of his estates at
Wressell and at Leconfield. There was still a sense that a gallant
man would follow, without questioning, the Percy leadership.

As the rebellion got under way the peaceful area could be defined. Thus the town of Newcastle-on-Tyne and Lord Cumberland's castle at Skipton-in-Craven were both held in the King's
interest. The Pilgrims never crossed the Pennine range. Regarded
from a sociological point of view the Pilgrimage of Grace can be
considered as the last but one of the seismic disturbances to affect
the North of England. The final episode would be the Northern
Rising of 1569 in the reign of Queen Elizabeth, when the power of
the Nevilles Earls of Westmorland was broken and the Percies
would be kept thenceforward in the South of England until the
end of the male line of that great house.

Neither of these rebellions affected Lancashire, although this was
to remain the most Catholic area in the northern counties. The
medieval nexus which can be traced both in the Pilgrimage and in
the Northern Rising was broken here. Catholicism was found en-
trenched among the small gentry and the yeomen and country
people in the Fylde and other areas of Lancashire, this was not
reflected among the heads of the one great family, the Earls of
Derby.

Edward Stanley third Earl of Derby was their chief for fifty
years from his accession in 1521 until his death in 1572. He had
inherited at thirteen and had been a ward of Cardinal Wolsey. He
was a man of conservative preferences as is shown by his votes in
the House of Lords in 1548 and 1552 in which he favoured the old-
fashioned Henrican views. He never opposed in any way the royal
policy either in the temporal or the religious spheres.[1] At one time

---

[1] For details of this Earl's later life cf. the Household Expenses of Edward Earl of
Derby for the year 1561 and his Household Regulations for 1568 printed in *The
Stanley Papers, Part 2* (Chetham Society), (1853), pp. 1–12.

Robert Aske had hoped to find some understanding for his point of view in the young Earl of Derby. It appears that there was actually no comprehension.

Meanwhile from all over England the levies organized by the gentry moved against the areas of disaffection. The core of the royal resistance depended upon the Talbots, George fourth Earl of Shrewsbury and his eldest son. They may be considered to have been the leaders of the old Conservative peerage. The Earl had inherited the headship of his great family long ago. The troubled later years of Edward IV and the reign of Richard III had passed in his minority. He had borne the sword *curtana* at the coronation of the first Tudor king; his whole life had been bound up with the new dynasty. His mother had been a Stafford, but he had long seen that his cousin the Duke of Buckingham was quite impracticable. He had lands in many parts of England, but his favoured residence was Sheffield Castle. He had held throughout the reign the great office of Lord Steward of the Household. It was natural that at the Duke of Buckingham's disaster he should be chosen as steward of his lands. He was throughout his life a great domestic courtier.

Although not himself a Yorkshireman, he could see from Sheffield Castle the whole of the lie of the North Country. He knew the Percies intimately. He was after all the father of the unfortunate Countess of Northumberland. Another great peer was also watching these events. The Earl of Rutland sat at Belvoir just beyond the southern borders of those Lincolnshire levels whose northern parishes were in revolt. He was a younger man than Shrewsbury and held the office of Warden of Sherwood Forest. In later life he would become Lord Chamberlain to the Queens Consort. He was now appointed as joint-commander with Shrewsbury of the royal levies.

It is important not to over-emphasize the element of armed conflict. Since the many bloody actions of the Wars of the Roses, which remained a recent and most unpleasant memory, the lords and indeed the gentlemen did not in effect make war on one another. What was now seen was a great gathering against the pilgrims led by all those who valued their association with the English Court.

The King necessarily employed the holders of the two surviving dukedoms. Charles Brandon, Duke of Suffolk was chosen first and was sent forward into Lincolnshire. He was at this time ageing and his great weight was beginning to tell on him. He had lost his wife the Queen of France in 1533 before the beginning of these troubles, and he had married again. His new wife had been left as the betrothed bride of his only son the Earl of Lincoln, who had died in adolescence. She was half-Spanish the daughter of Lord Willoughby by Queen Catherine's compatriot and friend Doña Maria de Salinas. Suffolk was weakening, but this could by no means be said of his colleague the Duke of Norfolk. The King had brought him forward with some reluctance from his snug retreat in his own county. Henry VIII still found distasteful the memory of the conduct of Anne Boleyn. The King's courtiers were thus all brought together to bring down His Grace's rebellious subjects.

There is one element that cannot be omitted in considering the outlook of the King's greatest subjects and that is the impending dissolution of all the monasteries. The lesser monasteries were already falling; but it was the greater houses whose properties would tempt the richer peers. The courtiers had been passive and now these gifts would come to them. There was nothing that they need do in this connection except to manifest their loyalty to their much-tried sovereign.

The wealthier earls had lands in several counties and each had a bureau for their administration. Without strain they could absorb the great areas of land which in this unexpected fashion now came before them. An example is provided in the case of the two peers who were the King's joint-generals. The Earl of Shrewsbury obtained the abbeys of Buildwas, Combermere, Shrewsbury, Welbeck and Wilton and the priories of Tutbury and Wenlock, and all their properties. The Earl of Rutland for his part received the religious houses and their lands of Beverley, Chartley, Croxton, Garradon, Nunburnholme, Warter and Rievaulx. In some cases the lands that thus accrued to both these earls were later sold or exchanged.

These factors are sufficient to explain the atmosphere of complaisance that bore down upon the great loyalists among the peers as they sat quietly at their wine at the high table beneath the Arras in Sheffield Castle. A very different state of mind must have existed among the draughty halls of Pontefract.

At Pontefract in that large gathering which was the final action of the Pilgrimage of Grace only two men really knew their royal master or had some measure of authority from him, Lord Darcy, who was governor of the King's castle at Pontefract, and the Northern Primate, Archbishop Lee. The Bishop of Durham had retreated to Norham Castle beyond their boundaries and the Earl of Northumberland was now dying. He lay at Wressell, 'his whole body as yellow as saffron'.

The great majority of the assembly had never seen their sovereign. The few who had done so only knew the King in his carefree days at the time of the Cloth of Gold; those days were past. The autumn mists wreathed round the old grey town. December rains poured down on Pontefract.

There had been a council at York and negotiations at Doncaster, the few peers who came now to Pontefract need only be mentioned to be dismissed. There was the boy Lord Neville and Lords Latimer and Lumley, the first was never charged and the second and third were freely pardoned. There were also Lord Conyers, a son-in-law of Lord Dacres of the North, and Lord Scrope of Bolton, a brother-in-law of the Earl of Cumberland. These, too, were pardoned and Lord Scrope later received monastic land.[1] There were also twenty-three knights and twenty-six gentlemen. Sir Thomas Percy was among those absent. Those present included Sir Ralph Filerker and Robert Bowes, who had alone gone to the Court and now had their pardons in their pockets.

Lord Darcy and Archbishop Lee, although at opposite ends of the political spectrum, were secret men and they were both in danger of ruin from the form that the rebellion had begun to take. Lord Darcy's career was long since over; his wives were dead. His son Sir Arthur Darcy, a prudent person, stood at some distance from him. Now he sat in his good house at Templehurst; it was autumn and the leaves were falling in his pleached avenues. The

---

[1] In December 1537 he received a thirty years' lease of the house and lands of the monastery of St Agatha at Easby, *Letters and Papers*, vol. XIII, part I, p. 588.

manor, like so many of that period in Yorkshire, has disappeared. It stood close to what was to be the Great Northern main line, where it runs to Scotland straight across the Selby levels.

Lord Darcy must by this time have suspected that his correspondence with the Imperial Ambassador was known and that in consequence he was already doomed. There seems something autumnal in his conversation. It was on 14 November that Somerset herald had come to him from the Duke of Suffolk at his own house.

A meticulous account of the conversation has been preserved. Immediately on his arrival the herald was taken through the hall into a parlour and thence into the chamber where Lord Darcy sat. His host removed his cap and took him by the hand. The herald explained that he had been sent by the King's lieutenant the Duke of Suffolk. Lord Darcy then carefully set out his defence. He explained that at the beginning of the Rising, 'I said to my friends and servants, sirs, we cannot do the King a greater service than to take this fellow [Aske]. . . . When I saw that I could not get him, and that the people did arise on every part, yea and further that I might not trust my own tenants, then I went with as many as I might get to the King's castle at Pontefract to keep and defend the same . . . and thither came to me the Archbishop of York and Master Magnus because I was an old man of war, that by my policy they might have escaped. They can bear record of all this that I show you.'

And then his explanation became more difficult. 'The captain [Aske],' he continued, 'wrote letters charging me upon pain of my life that I should yield the Castle. And if I would not, if they might take me by force they would slay me and all those that were with me and they would burn my houses [at Templehurst] and kill my son's children. For all that I could do with all the friends I could make, they would not respite me but till seven of the clock, then could I not hear nor see succour come and I had not in the Castle as much gunpowder as would fill a walnut nor so much fuel as would dress our supper, and further my victuals that should have come to me were eaten and drunk in the street before my face. I then being an old man of war . . . perceiving myself in that danger and could escape no otherwise with my life, for safeguard of the same did yield myself. I promise you if I had not wrought politically, it would have cost me my life.'[1]

There was not really very much more that Lord Darcy could bring forward. 'There is not man living,' he said bravely,[2] 'that shall be more ready to do His Grace's commandment than I, for if His Highness would command me to go with you his herald to defy the great Turk, by the faith that I owe to God and him I would do it with a good will, old as I am.' His servant brought the herald into a fair chamber where there was a good fire and gave him a venison pasty, bread, wine and beer. Lord Darcy gave the herald a double ducat and to Berwick pursuivant he gave an angel.[3] He then in time rode back to Pontefract; there was no outcome.

Archbishop Lee was a stranger in the northern province as his predecessors had often been. He was born in Kent, the son of a landowner at Lee Magna, who came of a rich mercantile stock. He had begun life at Magdalen, Wolsey's college. Dr Lee was a royal almoner and archdeacon of Colchester; he had held no pastoral charge. His only ecclesiastical supporter in his earlier life appears to have been Bishop Standish of St Asaph, an equivocal figure who attacked both More and Erasmus from the standpoint of a philistine conservative. For the most part his work was in diplomacy and his rewards were Church appointments. He was one of the very last bishops whom the Pope appointed, when Wolsey died; but the whole motive force of his career depended on his sovereign's wishes.

He was determined, as it was intended that he should be determined, never to suffer execution like the Bishop of Rochester. He would die in peace among his pillow cases. But this statement is in some ways unfair. Clerics of Archbishop Lee's school and generation neither liked nor admired old Bishop Fisher. Edward Lee was typical of those churchmen whose life was given to the service of the English Crown. His tastes were in some respects conservative; but the Papacy had been throughout his life and would remain at the periphery of his interests. He had been brought up to give

---

[1] Account printed in full in *The Pilgrimage of Grace*, I, pp. 300–6, cf. *Letters and Papers*, XI, 1059.
[2] *The Pilgrimage of Grace*, V, p. 304.   [3] *ibid.* , I, p. 306.

assent to all the Catholic arguments; but the position of the Bishop
of Rome is likely to have seemed to him strictly utilitarian.

Above all, as a leading royal officer alone in the wild North he
must have been lonely. He had at hand Archdeacon Magnus, a
survivor of the earlier Richmond administration, a Midland man
who had passed his life in the King's service. For the rest his clergy
were remote from him as they had been for generations from their
own archbishop. He had a great position as the Northern Primate
and he had here a flock deeply and perhaps superstitiously respectful, who hoped to work the oracle on their own behalf. In the
South there was the King by whom it was important to be liked,
but who, as Dr Lee well knew, had no warmth towards him.

In the first days of the rebellion the Archbishop had made some
statements that savoured of imprudence; but now he was surrounded by the Pilgrims, while the forces of the kingdom were
dressed against them. At this period of the gathering at Pontefract
he was asked to gain opinions from the clergy and he established
himself in the priory there. Many of the northern priests had
gathered round him. Lord Darcy was in the castle and it was
evident that he must steer quite clear of that ill-omened figure.

The Archbishop was, as has been said, a secret man and this
must explain why he was invited to preach in public to the
assembled Pilgrims. It is by no means evident why he was asked
to make an open statement. He preached[1] at Mass in the parish
church at Pontefract on the morning of Sunday, 3 December. His
text has not been preserved, but he began his sermon by speaking
of the sacraments of baptism, penance and communion. He then
stated that lands given to the Church might not be put to profane
uses and that priests ought not to fight in any circumstances. He
was about to describe the name and nature of a 'peregrynage',
when Lancaster herald came into the church. There was now
present an expert and so-to-speak a neutral witness. After a pause
the Archbishop declared that the Faith had been sufficiently determined in the King's Book of Articles, that the sword was given to
none but a prince and that no man should draw it but by his
prince's orders.

The body of the church was crowded with divines and gentle-

---

[1] A detailed account of this sermon is given in *The Pilgrimage of Grace*, I, pp. 377–82.

L: Chancelor

20 Richard, Lord Rich

Tho: Wiatt Knight.

21 Sir Thomas Wyatt

men and the commons had been packed into the gallery at the
west end. The commons began an uproar and Aske and his immediate companions hurried the Archbishop away. It must have
been clear to him that he had now saved himself. He rode back to
Cawood in quietude. He had still seven years of life ahead of him,
a rather old-fashioned celibate ecclesiastic. Strains could come
suddenly upon one in King Henry's reign. It is worth noting that
Cromwell, who was cordial to all men who would work with him,
now stood his friend.

K

IX

The Exeter Conspiracy

The destruction of the White Rose family was absolutely distinct from the Pilgrimage of Grace, but it is linked with it in that the execution of the Countess of Salisbury was the direct result of Sir John Neville's action, the last and the least effective of the different stirs in the North Country. As so often in King Henry's reign the attack on the last surviving of the royal stocks came out of a clear sky. For meanwhile the situation had improved greatly for the royal cause. In October 1537 Queen Jane gave birth to a Prince of Wales. Soon afterwards the Queen had a relapse. She made her confession and received the last sacraments and on 24 October she died. The King's elder daughter the Princess Mary was the chief mourner at her funeral. England now had a united royal family.

Henceforward there was an undoubted legitimate heir to the Crown, Edward the Prince of Wales. There was also a new factor in the field of politics, Edward's uncle, Edward Seymour, the Earl of Hertford, who would remain a figure of steadily growing influence throughout the reign. He was in fact a new phenomenon, something that would come to fruition in the later reigns of Edward VI and Elizabeth, the Protestant courtier. When this element developed it is difficult to say for he knew how to conduct himself in that strange *milieu*. He was a young man and both grave and silent. He had been about the Court since childhood and was the only man with whom Cromwell sought to ally himself in marriage. This was not so very significant for all that Seymour could offer to the older statesman was fair weather friendship.

Already in these years 1537 and 1538 the leading figures about the King were ageing, while he himself was growing tired and his suppurating leg was always painful. Cromwell himself was growing old and so were his two principal opponents the Duke of Norfolk and Bishop Gardiner, and it was one of the King's rather human traits that he did not care so much for ageing men. Meanwhile there was so much to do and it fell to the Lord Privy Seal to do it.

The younger generation was now growing up including the Duke of Norfolk's elder son the Earl of Surrey. It was in most ways a happy time to be at Court for the great monastic lands were now available. Never before had there been such unlooked for and improbable opportunities.

After the Pilgrimage of Grace it must have seemed inevitable to the watchful onlooker that disaster was bound to come upon the White Rose family. With the passage of the years they had become more isolated than the other stocks which gathered round King Henry's Court. The Courtenays in particular had no near relatives. The Marquess of Exeter had been an only child; the little Lord Courtenay was the sole issue of his second marriage. Whatever the King felt about Lord Exeter, his wife had always been too close to the Dowager Princess of Wales. Some efforts had been made to test out the peer himself. He had been asked to sign the letter to the Pope in favour of the plea for a divorce. He acted as a commissioner for Queen Catherine's deposition and as a member of the Court which tried Anne Boleyn; he was high steward at the trial of Lord Darcy and Lord Hussey. In return he was offered some monastic land. All this had been accepted with passivity.

He had great estates in the western counties. It was these, perhaps, which caused the Government to determine to settle their accounts with him. Lord Exeter did not then live on his properties in Devonshire, but divided his time between his house at Horsley in Surrey and his London mansion, the Red Rose. The Marquess was not in general interested in books, but was accustomed to study a fine volume with the arms of the Knights of the Garter very beautifully tricked out. Jugglers appealed to him and he liked to watch displays of wrestling and to hear his servants 'sing properly in three-man songs'. His wife's attendants played skilfully upon the virginals. He maintained serious good relations with his chaplains and among his equals his chief intimate seems to have been Lord Delawarr.

The Countess of Salisbury, the only surviving child of the Duke of Clarence, was now sixty-five, had been a widow for thirty years and was the mother of the Poles. She lived at Warblington[1] in Hampshire with a considerable establishment amid an atmosphere of hearty devotion. Three chaplains were in residence. Her freedom of speech was characteristic of her strong-minded independence. She was prepared to swear by her damnation when it was necessary to enforce a serious point. Almost throughout his life Lord Exeter retained the constableship of Windsor Castle and both the Courtenays and the Poles attended the great functions of the Court until the end.

There were certain differences between the position of these two families. The Courtenays had that long-established property which was a smaller version of the great Buckingham inheritance, which had aroused the King's suspicions. On the other hand they had no claim whatever to the throne as long as the King and his two sisters lived and had issue. This was because their sole claim was derived from the Marquess of Exeter's mother the Lady Catherine, who was the younger sister of Queen Elizabeth, Henry VII's wife.

The position of the Poles was stronger as regards a claim to the royal succession for the Countess of Salisbury was the sole heiress of Edward IV's brother the Duke of Clarence.[2] On the other hand while the Courtenays had been quite aloof from the Duke of Buckingham, a situation which was emphasized when they received a small portion of his attainted lands, the Poles had been closely linked with him. Lady Salisbury's only daughter had been married to Lord Stafford, the Duke's only son. Still, the whole of Lady Salisbury's estates had been granted or for the greater part more accurately re-granted to her by the reigning King. She was the Governess of the Princess Mary.

When she was created Countess of Salisbury in 1513, her eldest son who was then just of age was raised to the peerage as Lord

---

[1] The remains of the brick entrance gate-way to Warblington still survives among farm buildings.

[2] It will be recalled that if Richard III's contention that his elder brother's children were illegitimate should be correct, Lady Salisbury would on her brother's death in 1499 have become the heir general of the House of York.

Montagu.[1] He was married to the daughter of Lord Abergavenny, the head of the southern branch of the House of Neville, a religious woman. She always retained her *penchant* for alliances with such high stocks. As late as 1534 her granddaughter Catherine, who was Montagu's heiress, was married to the boy Lord Hastings, the Earl of Huntingdon's young heir. The strange factor in this last alliance is that Huntingdon did not consider that it was dangerous to ally himself with Lady Salisbury, who was by that time falling into the King's disfavour.

The fall and destruction of her house came from her single-minded affection for Reginald Pole, her younger son. Lady Salisbury's husband,[2] a shadowy figure, had died before December 1505; she alone steered her family's course. The difficulties with the Government arose at the end of August 1538 and these were the result of the actions of Reginald Pole.

Lady Salisbury had hoped from his childhood onwards to build a great ecclesiastical career for him, something like that of her uncle Archbishop Neville or her cousin Cardinal Bourchier. Like other members of her stock, the temper of her mind reposed at ease upon the previous century. The King's goodwill made the first steps in this matter very simple for her.

Reginald Pole was born in March 1500. He was first sent to school to the charterhouse at Sheen and then to the house of the Carmelite friars at Oxford; he matriculated as a nobleman at Magdalen College. Meanwhile his mother had obtained for him the deanery of the collegiate church of Wimborne Minster and the two prebends of Boscombe and Yatminster Secunda, both in Salisbury Cathedral. As soon as he came of age he was sent at his own wish and at the King's expense to study in Padua. While abroad he was appointed Dean of Exeter in 1527, the year of his return. In 1529 he went with the King's permission and at his expense to Paris for a year.

Henry recalled him in July 1530 and until January 1532 he re-

[1] Lady Salisbury's claim to this title came through her mother the Duchess of Clarence who was the senior co-heiress of the Montagus, Earls of Salisbury, hence also the title chosen for her eldest son.

[2] Sir Richard Pole was at the time of his marriage Constable of Harlech Castle and Sheriff for life of Merioneth. He later, in 1499, received the Garter. He was the son of Sir Geoffrey Pole of Medmenham by his wife Edith St John, who was half-sister through her mother to Margaret Beaufort.

mained in England living for the most part in the charterhouse of
Sheen. By this time it was clear that separation from Rome was in
prospect and when the King offered him either the archbishopric
of York or the bishopric of Winchester, both vacant by Wolsey's
death, Reginald Pole refused the offers. Given his convictions,
these refusals were inevitable for either post would have involved
following his sovereign into a separation from the Roman Church.
He went abroad and did not return to England for a quarter of a
century.

When I first worked on this subject I was attracted by his role in
later life when he was, under Queen Mary, the last Archbishop of
Canterbury in communion with the Holy See. His earlier career
now seems to me less sympathetic. He went to Italy, took part
against the King and accepted the cardinalate. It was this ac-
ceptance which would bring his family down. It is possible that he
could have gone back to Padua, lived quietly and refused promotion. Of course his kitchen would have been haunted by Cromwell's
spies; but if he had lived in peace and held no correspondence
with the Vatican they would have had nothing to report against
him. And then, of course, his family in England might have survived. Still this idea is based on a Victorian conception of family
life; it is anachronistic when considering a Tudor household.

In the event he went to Rome and on 22 December 1536 he was
raised to the Sacred College as Cardinal Deacon of Santa Maria in
Cosmedin. It is worth noting that for another twenty years he
would not be a priest. He soon began his fruitless work as a papal
legate. He was slender and of middle height with a flowing light
brown beard and very serious. His eyes were blue-grey and rather
small. Like many another ecclesiastic, his strong point was not his
imagination. He had been brought up in the high privileged circles
of the old world from whose values he never really freed himself.
Much flattery was paid to him on account of his birth and his
exalted station. He was in fact an honest pious man of studious
temperament with little knowledge of the modern world.

There was, however, another side to Reginald Pole's character.
He was an intimate of the learned Cardinal Contarini and left
many writings including the *De Unitate Ecclesiastica*. These do not
seem to have affected his appreciations of the English scene.

The new Cardinal's journey as a papal legate was certainly ill-conceived; but one can hardly blame the Farnese Pope for he knew nothing about Pole's country. Both the King of France and the Queen of Hungary, who was Governess of the Netherlands for the Emperor, had the prudence to refuse him. He found refuge with the Cardinal de la Marck, who was independent prince Bishop of Liège. He set off from Rome as soon as the Pilgrimage of Grace was over. It did not prove a successful expedition and after his return Cardinal Pole remained for many years quietly anchored at the Papal Court.

Nevertheless this northern journey was sufficient to bring down his family. They had done what they could to disavow him; but in the year that followed the failure of the Pilgrimage of Grace the prudent men avoided them. Lady Salisbury lived at Warblington and Lord Montagu at Buckmere in the Thames valley. At the end of August 1538 Sir Geoffrey Pole, the youngest son of this family was arrested on a charge of holding illicit communication with the Cardinal. Under pressure he gave evidence which put his brother and cousin within reach of the law and a combing of the household at Horsley provided further data from among the one hundred and thirty Courtenay dependents. After allowance has been made in regard to their accuracy, these depositions still give an impression of the character of the discontent. Lord Montagu was accused of saying[1] that 'he trusted to see the abbeys up again one day' and Lord Delawarr had backed up this statement. 'A time will come,' he was reported[2] to have said, 'that God will punish for the pulling down of abbeys and for reading of these new English books.' George Croftes, Chancellor of Chichester Cathedral confessed that he had encouraged such scruples. 'When the statute was made for the abolishment of the Bishop of Rome's authority this examinate,' he declared,[3] 'once showed the Lord Delawarr that it was a mad thing to go about by making of a law to make men believe that in England the contrary whereof was belived in all places of the world.'

Lord Delawarr is a shadowy figure, remembered now for the

---

[1] *Letters and Papers*, XIII, ii, n. 827, examination of John Collins.
[2] *ibid.*, n. 831, examination of Sir Hugh Owen.
[3] *ibid.*, n. 827, examination of Chancellor Croftes.

beautiful chantry in the Italian style, with a mixture of Gothic and Renaissance detail, that he erected as late as 1532 for his wife and himself in the priory church of St Mary and St Blaise at Boxgrave in Sussex. His reactions appear typical of an old-fashioned conservative peer in the South Country. His father had been an early supporter of Henry VII and had obtained much of the Sussex lands of the attainted Dukes of Norfolk, including St Leonard's Forest and the Howard property in the Rape of Bramber. He himself lived at Halnaker House, the inheritance of his wife, a Bonville heiress. He obtained leave of absence from attending Parliament in 1532 on the alleged grounds of his poverty. He died at peace in the reign of Queen Mary in 1554.

In his fifth examination Sir Geoffrey Pole described how when riding between London and Horsley, the Lord Marquis had said that he had been compelled to leave his constableship of Windsor and to take abbey lands instead. 'What,' Sir Geoffrey had exclaimed,[1] 'be you come to this point to take abbey lands now?' 'Yes,' said he, 'good enough for a time. They must have all again one day.'

And then Lady Exeter confessed that she had discussed the question of those rebellions from which her House had kept free. 'Madam,' Sir Edward Neville had said to her in reference to the Pilgrimage of Grace,[2] 'be afeard not of this, nor of the second but beware of the third.' She professed to have feared the development of some conspiracy of Lord Abergavenny's family. 'Ah, Mr Neville,' she had replied, 'you will never leave off your Welsh prophecies, but one day this will turn to your displeasure.' Exeter and Montagu were executed, Lady Exeter and Lady Salisbury imprisoned and the Lady Salisbury was beheaded two years later after the failure of Sir John Neville's stir.

After the attainders just described, the King's Councillors became more pliant, judicious in their outlook and accommodating. They were ready to obey their sovereign and to destroy, restore or modify the Catholic forms.

It may be said that there was a difference in the nature of the attacks on the two White Rose families. Cardinal Pole's activity

---

[1] *ibid.*, n. 804, examination of Sir Geoffrey Pole.
[2] *ibid.*, n. 804, examination of the Marchioness of Exeter.

was sufficient to bring his own relatives into suspicion; but the accusations made against the Marquess of Exeter were rather different. It appears likely that it was Lady Exeter, who was whole-hearted in opposition, Cromwell had a desire to clear away the dead wood of the fifteenth century.

A couple of memoranda will reveal the sleepless vigilance of the Privy Seal. The first runs,[1] 'To the Egyptians and what shall be done with them. The letters and news from Venice. To know whether the King will have the birds from Canaria.' The second contains these sentences,[2] 'To send a commission for the Egyptians in the West. To remember the Lady Marchioness of Exeter. To remember the two children (Edward Courtenay and Henry Pole) in the Tower. Whether the King will have the birds of Canaria.'

[1] *Letters and Papers*, vol. XIV, part 2, 1539, p. 175.
[2] *ibid.*, p. 176.

X

A Group of Courtiers

There was a group of adherents who through the years had become associated with King Henry's Court. A study of this grouping shows most of all the profound dominance of the King's character. These men had all throughout their period of service become accustomed to mould their wishes to the King's desires. He had been a young sovereign with ordinary tastes and a superficial cheerfulness. It does not seem to have occurred to him that his will could be crossed by those who had received his kindly favour. As a consequence the closer that a man might be to his King the less imaginable would it seem that he should ever oppose his royal master. King Henry saw no reason to exercise forgiveness in regard to those close to him who disobeyed him. Nor was it hard for those belonging to the Court to practice this obedience. The Reforming years came very smoothly. So far as men desired the accustomed practice of the life of their religion this remained open to them. It was natural for a courtier to support his King in any quarrel with the papal monarchy. And then there came upon them this rain of gold, the profits of the great monastic properties.

Chief among the first set of courtiers to be considered there were the half-brothers Sir William Fitzwilliam and Sir Anthony Browne, the former better known as the Earl of Southampton of the first creation. Like Charles Brandon, with whom they were connected, these two would pass their entire lives in the royal service and derived their whole great properties from the King's favour. They may perhaps be conceived as men of no great imagination who were polarized at each point of their career to the King's wishes. It is also worth noting, but should not be overstressed, that they had their own connection with the royal stock, for Sir Thomas Fitzwilliam of Aldwarkes in the West Riding and Sir Anthony Browne, the royal standard bearer, were the successive husbands of Lady Lucy Neville one of the daughters of John Marquess of Montagu.[1] There was, however, no financial backing for Lady Lucy did not marry until her father had been killed and his goods confiscated.

William Fitzwilliam had joined the Court when he was ten and had become an Esquire of the Body to the sovereign in 1511 and Sir Anthony received the same office in 1524. They were thus very near to their sovereign and had an affinity that was unbreakable. Sir William the elder was the more important. He followed a naval career in so far as that was then practicable. He had been a commander at sea in 1513 and was named Vice-Admiral of England the next year. It is in this connection that he is mentioned in the accounts of the Field of the Cloth of Gold.

At the same time he was employed in many embassies and was Lord High Admiral from 1535 till 1540. In 1537 he had been created Earl of Southampton. Two years later his half-brother Sir Anthony Browne became Master of the Horse. These three men the Duke of Suffolk, Lord Southampton and Anthony Browne can be seen as examples of the most intimate among the King's older courtiers. To each of them it would be clear that the variations of the royal policy were of small importance. It does not appear that the religious problem seemed significant. They depended on their sovereign who had 'created' them and must stay close to him. The two elder were his contemporaries and were to die within the reign. Sir Anthony Browne survived him for a few months.

Both brothers were established in Sussex, in the eastern and western portions of that county. Sir Anthony received the great monastery of Battle Abbey, where he kept and adapted the abbot's lodging and razed the rest. He also obtained the priory of St Mary Overy in Southwark. He cleared the ground there and built a town house for his family. Sir William Fitzwilliam purchased the estate of Cowdray, which had belonged to Sir David Owen. During the years he was at work on Cowdray House, building the large six-sided tower at the northern end of the present ruins, the embattled parapets and the gate house and by about 1539 he had completed the beautiful and elaborate fan-vaulting of the porch.

[1] The Duke of Suffolk's second wife was her sister Lady Margaret Mortimer.

Through the great windows the tempered sunlight fell on the big portrait[1] by Holbein of Lord Southampton, a substantial figure holding the admiral's staff with its golden knob and in the background the sea.

In neither case was there any original inheritance. Monastic lands were granted to sustain this new-found property; for Sir William the lands of Waverley Abbey and those of the monasteries of Easebourne and Bayhurst and of the little priory with an odd name, Calceto outside Arundel. Sir Anthony for his part also gained property in the valley of the Brede and a portion of the old town of Hastings. Throughout this southern county the rich had found an ever-deepening peace.

Among the older generation of what can roughly be called the King's senior courtiers there were one or two who do not seem to fit in any category. Thus the third Lord Hastings belonged by marriage and inheritance to that section of the baronage closely associated with the Duke of Buckingham, whose sister he had married. At the same time he had gained his sovereign's liking. He had quarrelled with his wife, whose *liaison* with Sir William Compton had become public. He was extravagant and the King was generous to him. He was about three years Henry's senior. He had always been about the Court and had been made a knight of the Bath when he was thirteen. In 1529 the King advanced him to be Earl of Huntingdon. It is not easy to detect his personality. Like his contemporaries, who have been mentioned, he died before the King, in 1545.

A man of enterprise, who was attached in a more subordinate capacity to the King's entourage was Thomas Wriothesley. Like the two brothers, he in time acquired a great property, monastic in origin on the coasts of the South Country. He came of an undistinguished family known to the Court as heralds: his uncle of the same names was Garter king. He entered when quite young into Cromwell's personal service and was transferred about 1530 to the group which formed the King's own secretariate. He was born in 1505 and was in no sense at this stage one of the royal intimates, but his rise was steady. His area of gain was centred upon Southampton Water. He acquired from Quarr Abbey some

---

[1] Cf. the portrait of Holbein reproduced facing p. 129.

manors in the Isle of Wight and then the great properties in Hampshire of Beaulieu Abbey and Titchfield on either side of the tidal
stream.

This was an instance of a great grant of land preceding rather
than following the development of political significance. He was
close in to where the carving-up was taking place. Wriothesley's
period of power belonged to the last years of the King's reign;
when he became Lord Chancellor and received the Garter. By the
wish of Henry VIII expressed before his death, he was created
Earl of Southampton of the second creation. We shall come upon
his actions at a later stage.

Great lawyers also obtained monastic properties in the Home
Counties at this time. Thus the two who have obtained such re-
probation for their attacks on Thomas More, received great
monasteries in Essex. Both were conveniently near to London for
the headquarters of a noble stock. Sir Thomas Audley became
Lord Audley of Walden taking his title from that monastery on
whose site was later built the great house of Audley End. Sir
Richard Rich, who reached the Woolsack and was chancellor of
augmentations,[1] came of a mercer's family in the City and established himself at Lees or Leigh's Priory in Essex. In this case he
took over the prior's lodgings and other parts of the house for his
own use.[2]

Lord Rich has been attacked beyond measure by Victorian
historians because he took part in the Government's actions against
Thomas More. For a lawyer who would not surrender his ambi-
tions there was no alternative that was open to him. He had a
dislike for monks and the Papacy meant nothing to him. As far as
religious observances were concerned, he had a very mild preference for the ancient customs; but his real interests lay in very
different matters. His fortune came entirely from the law and from
the City; his wife had brought him a heavy dowry from the
Grocers' Company. He was bedding all this out to make a landed
family. In this way the years went by contentedly. He seems to
have had no interest in the King's taste for sport or in his world.
He built with foresight through the happy years, and at the end he

---

[1] He held this office from 1538 until 1544.
[2] There was a three-storeyed gate house here as at Coughton and Layer Marney.

had created Felsted School. In his great hall, as in Lord Southampton's, there hung one of Holbein's finest portraits.[1] Sir Richard looked out very calm and tranquil. I admit that it is an unusual reading of his character and I make it tentatively.

It is also worth noting that nothing could interfere with the slow accretions of the landed polity. Thus Lord Audley of Walden left no sons. The heir to his property was a tiny girl. Her new estates now lay to the westward of the Howard agglomeration. It could have been foreseen that in later years her property would pass through marriage to the Dukes of Norfolk.

Apart from those who joined the King's service when quite young, there were others who also had a quiet passage. For the most part these were men who had their origin in the greater squirearchy. Lord St John of Basing is a good example. Both his parents were members of the Paulet family, his mother coming from the branch which built the great Tudor house at Hinton St George in the south of Somerset. From his father Sir John Paulet, he inherited the estate on which he later built his own famous mansion Basing House. He was a friend and neighbour of Lord Sandys of the Vyne and began his career, like him, on county business. He was older than the King and made forward peacefully throughout the reign. He was master of the royal wards in 1526 and joined the privy council. In 1532 he became comptroller of the royal household and shared with Thomas Cromwell the mastership of the King's woods. He obtained the possessions of Netley Abbey near Southampton when the monastic lands came on the market. He was so cautious that he was little noticed. Like Wriothesley his career developed in the last years of the reign. It seems that for a man already careful, it was of great assistance to repose upon the influence of the richer gentry. Among all the great men of this period the Marquess of Winchester, as he became in time, was the least the architect of his own fortune.

Among the lesser courtiers the acquisition of a suppressed monastery seems almost common form. Sir William Kingston may be taken as an example. He had been sent up North to arrest Wolsey and was constable of the Tower when Anne Boleyn was confined there. He came of a landed family from Painswick in

[1] Cf. the portrait by Holbein reproduced facing p. 144.

Gloucestershire and received a grant of the Cistercian abbey of Flaxley in the same county. In fact it is difficult to find those about the Court who had no share in the harvest. Thomas second Lord Vaux of Harrowden[1] may have belonged to this small grouping: but our information is really insufficient and it is always difficult to prove a negative.

More perhaps than any others of this grouping, Sir Thomas Wyatt[2] had had his own career carved out for him. His chief distinction, which was that of a poet, was irrelevant to the development of his worldly success. He seems to have been without mundane ambition. He lacked that carefulness which was a trait of nearly all of his contemporaries, who made their fortunes. The King through his early years and, more surprisingly, his father both had gratitude, a virtue rather rare in a great sovereign. The Wyatt family ancestry is quite obscure, but Sir Thomas's father Henry Wyatt was a supporter of the Earl of Richmond, who was released from imprisonment in the Tower of London after the victory of Bosworth Field. Sir Thomas was born in 1503 and there was never a moment when the King was unaware of him. In his career two points are worth considering, his outlook on religion and on marital fidelity.

In this matter of religion the three generations of the Wyatt family had each their different emphasis. Sir Thomas in a letter[3] to his son described his father, 'his great reverence for God . . . no man more pitiful, no man diligenter, nore more circumspect'. One should not perhaps read too much into the word 'circumspect'; but it does seem to reflect the Catholic sovereigns Henry VII of England and Louis XI in whose lives were entangled both piety and dissimulation.

In Sir Henry's grandson, Sir Thomas the younger, a Protestant emphasis is clearly seen, while in Sir Thomas the elder we come upon a clear indifference. It is, perhaps, pretentious to describe this as Agnosticism; but it may serve to explain one of the links which bound him to Thomas Cromwell. The question of his marriage has its own importance. This took place when he was seven-

---

[1] Cf. the portrait by Holbein reproduced facing p. 33.
[2] Cf. Holbein's drawing of Sir Thomas Wyatt reproduced facing p. 145.
[3] Letter dated 15 April 1537, cf. Patricia Thomson, *Sir Thomas Wyatt and His Background* (1964), p. 3.

teen and the bride was Elizabeth Brooke daughter of Lord Cobham. The following year she gave birth to her son the second Sir
Thomas Wyatt. At some time in the succeeding years he parted
from his wife charging her with misconduct. In 1537 he refused to
maintain his separated wife and forced her to return to her own
family. It is worth noting that the use of the archdiocesan court of
Canterbury for marriage cases in the years following the breach
with Rome does not yet appear to have been studied. An almost
parallel case concerning a man of the same rank is that of Sir
Edward Seymour,[1] later the Protector Somerset. Such difficulties
were wholly unconnected with religious changes; they were
merely the results of an atavistic determination of the landed
gentry that no wife should bring a bastard son into their own
stock.

Through these years Thomas Wyatt would remain an unchaste
husband and in the widest sense a true anti-clerical. He also had,
so it seems to me, a profound indifference to any question of religion which was a point of view that is found at this time in France,
but was quite rare in England. He was the heir to the castle and
estate of Allington on the Medway, which his father had purchased in 1492. Sir Henry had been knighted and had become a
privy councillor and treasurer of the King's Chamber. He had
made the way for his only son. The young Thomas held a minor
office at the Court as clerk to the King's Jewels. In 1525 he was an
Esquire of the Body. He received the abbey of Boxley, the site of
the Boxley Rood, which stood quite near his father's property.

Wyatt's alleged relations with Anne Boleyn, formed a cedilla to
her destruction. The various references to her in Wyatt's verse
have concentrated attention on this point. He was only twenty-
one when he first came to Court at a time when the young Anne
Boleyn, who was his neighbour at Hever Castle and a cousin of his
own wife, had only just come back from the Court of France. It
appears to me unlikely that he ever had any sexual relations with
Anne Boleyn. At any rate he withdrew when once it became clear
that she had gained her sovereign's interest. Such a withdrawal

---

[1] Seymour had married Catherine Fillol and in these same years he repudiated her
on the ground of misconduct with her father-in-law. His second marriage took place
in 1536. There is, however, a doubt as to whether his repudiated wife was living at the
date of his second marriage.

would be both a prudent and suitable action on the part of a young courtier. He still had his contacts with the Court and he felt the backwash of the disaster which overcame her and her favoured friends. He was placed in the Tower for a brief time and then sent back to Allington, his father's house.

In all these matters the most important of all men stood his friend, Thomas Cromwell. It may well have been a relief to the elder statesman heavily involved in the religious changes and surrounded by the Henrican clergy to have this one younger intimate who was free from any interest in such affairs. Wyatt reached the privy council in 1533 and had been knighted four years later. He was now embarked on a diplomatic career under the Lord Privy Seal's direction. His portrait by Holbein dated from this time. As his career went forward it is worth noting that Wyatt had another patron besides Cromwell. He had always maintained a reverent respect for the Duke of Norfolk, who was godfather to his only son.

A letter written in 1540 reveals a clear impression of his outlook. 'Come on now, my Lord of London,' he wrote to Bishop Bonner,[1] 'what is my abominable and vicious living. Do you know it or have you heard it? I grant I do not profess chastity, but yet I use not abomination. If you know it, tell it here, with whom and when. If you heard it, who is your author? Have you seen me have any harlot in my house whilst you were in my company.' Perhaps none of the Henrican courtiers stood so far removed from all the clergy. At a later stage in the reign we shall come upon him again.

Throughout these years the Duke of Norfolk had been active in the King's concerns. At Kenninghall he took his view over East Anglia. 'I have never,' he wrote to Cromwell,[2] 'laboured to any but you, for the time of serving is at hand, and every nobleman doth clutch his portion. I trust well for Bungay and Wadebridge.' He knew very well the value of each former monastery.

And in the background there was always Thomas Cromwell. He alone was the active agent in those great events of which the courtiers were the passive beneficiaries. It was possible throughout these years, once Anne Boleyn was dead, that the King might re-

---

[1] See Wyatt's *Defence* against the Bishop of London's charge of loose living January 1541.
[2] Letter dated 10 September 1536, *Letter and Papers*, p. 173.

turn to his spiritual allegiance. It was also true that in all that great kaleidoscope of the English Court such change would make but little difference. Former monastic land would never have to leave its new possessors. There were only two great men whose careers could not survive a reconciliation with the Roman See, one was Cranmer, the King's archbishop of Canterbury and the other was Cromwell, the King's Vicar General in Spirituals.

Cromwell was in effect the universal legatee to Cardinal Wolsey; but it was his mistake that he never came close enough to his own sovereign. The whole manner of his life was truly sedentary. There is no evidence that he ever visited the Midlands or the North of England. He was wholly centred upon London; in some ways he can be considered as the very first of the great Londoners. Some aspects of his life are well reflected in a series of letters that he received when he was removed from London for a little while because the plague was in the air. He was informed by John Williams[1] that one of the masons dwelling against the great gate of Friars Austin was dead of the 'common sickness'. Williams was examining his various houses. 'I have viewed,' wrote his agent Thomas Croke,[2] 'your house at Hackney. The kitchen is finished except the paving. The wet and dry larders and the filling of the pool in the garden are well forward.' A little later John Williams wrote to him.[3] 'Your place at Hackney is in a good stay, except the garden which is a-digging.'

The most detailed account was sent to him by Thomas Thacker. This described[4] both the Austin Friars and Hackney and also the house that he was constructing at Stepney to be a residence for his nephew Richard Cromwell. It is worth stressing the middle class character of his whole background, all the more noticeable because he was at this time much sought after. The same summer he was invited by the Duke of Suffolk to join himself with the King as godfather to his own eldest son.[5]

'Your households,' began Thomas Thacker,[6] 'at the Rolls, Friars Austin, Hackney and Stepneth are in good health. The

---

[1] *Letters and Papers*, vol. IX, no. 413.   [2] *ibid.*, no. 272.   [3] *ibid.* no. 339.
[4] *Letters and Papers*, vol. IX.
[5] Charles later second Duke of Suffolk. His elder half-brother Henry Earl of Lincoln had died in 1534.
[6] *vere* Stepney.

stairs (in this last house) from your lodging down to the gallery is finished with a window where the jakes, was, very well done. Your building at Hackney goes forward, the brickwork of the kitchen with the chimney is finished to the roof; the roof set up and tiles upon it; the enlarging of the buttery and scullery brought above the ground. The roofs thereof are framing with all speed; your lodgings trimmed with windows, glass and hangings – a goodly place, in my opinion.'

He then describes the changes carried out at Friars Austin. 'The wall of the kitchen towards the street, the windows of freestone, with the scullery and other offices is clearly finished. The carpenter is raising the roofs and all is complete except the windows of the side of the hall towards the court. Your own lodging, with the chamber and the gallery above, are finished and plastered and want only glazing.'

There are then plans for a country house. This was to be at Ewhurst, a lonely parish lying under Leith Hill and to the south of it. 'On Sunday last,' we read, 'I went to Ewhurst and viewed there the goodly frames. The double floors of your hall and solar under it are finished. Certain goods must be transported to Ewhurst from the Thames waterside. Carriage is scarce because of hay time and harvest, but the parson of Ewhurst says that we shall have the carts next week.' They had received six hundred loads of brick and he had been paid by Wilson and Christopher Roper £100 on the Lord Privy Seal's behalf. One can understand that an isolated priest would wish to please the King's Vicar General in Spirituals.

There is a letter from Cromwell's intimate associate Stephen Vaughan. 'I fear,' he explains, 'that these great humidities will engender pestilence at the end of the year rather after Bartholomewtide than before it. Your old servant Williamson, in whom you have a jewel, spares no trouble.'

XI

The Fall of Cromwell

On 17 April 1540, when the Easter festivities were over and a new Parliament had lately met, Cromwell the Lord Privy Seal was promoted Earl of Essex and made Great Chamberlain of England. This was a great earldom which had only recently become extinct on the death of Henry Bourchier, the last of that ancient family and the representative of Thomas of Woodstock, Duke of Gloucester, the youngest son of Edward III. He had died when nearly seventy years of age from a broken neck the result of a fall from a German horse.

In connection with this Parliament an important service was required of Cromwell, a further exercise of his capacity for rendering the Houses first pliable and then generous in their money grants. Cromwell had held for five years the post of Vicar-General and Vicegerent of the King in Spirituals, and the promotions of this April marked the culminating point of a career characterized by a highly developed sense of politics, a clear grasp of state-craft, and a rapid, tortuous, supple mind. A list of his other posts and appointments reflect his predominance. He was Chancellor of the Exchequer and a Knight of the Garter, Chancellor and High Steward of the University of Cambridge, Warden and Chief Justice in eyre north of Trent, Governor of the Isle of Wight, Recorder of Bristol, a Privy Councillor of course and, rather surprisingly for so anti-clerical a layman, Dean of Wells. His post of visitor-general of the monasteries, absorbed in higher office, had become a sinecure, since the work of the total suppression of the religious houses had been carried through with smooth efficiency and was now almost completed. He had, indeed, deserved well of his sovereign.

It was, however, the very successful completion of his work which made Cromwell's position now precarious. He had become less necessary, and a man so hated could not survive once he had become unnecessary to his master. And Henry VIII was painfully accessible, desperately open to gusts of influence. The King might not be prepared to sacrifice anything of importance, but he would sacrifice an unprofitable servant.

Cromwell in April 1540 was already fighting a losing battle. The days of his first secure period of office were now behind him. He was fifty-five and had been for seven years the most powerful factor in English politics. Each year his responsibilities had increased and with them his pensioners and his beneficiaries and, of course, his enemies. He had long been an isolated man with a too-great knowledge of his world. His personal contacts were numerous and unexpected; many were valuable, some were painful, none was entirely frank. The legislative side of all his actions was most respectable and open to the public gaze. But there was always the more private side to his financial transactions. It is difficult for a moneylender to grow old gracefully.

Besides, Cromwell had first appeared in a rather menial capacity in the service of the Marquess of Dorset, and he had not the protection of the Church to make his rise to power less unacceptable. His great position in the State had made the lords and the churchmen approach him humbly and obsequiously. They were determined that Cromwell should one day pay for their obsequiousness.

The dissolution of the monasteries had come to the courtiers as an unhoped for piece of good fortune. Once they had found the easy terms on which great areas of well-developed property were obtainable, they entered with a serene calculation upon the golden age of the English landed interest. They reaped great profits without labour. Cromwell, on the other hand, carrying through his own plans, concentrated the opposition upon himself. Whatever little odium might attach in Court circles to the executions of the abbots of Colchester and Glastonbury was centred upon him. He received the blame for all the acts of oppression which were required before the monastery lands in the Kingdom could be parcelled out at moderate prices. The anger of the country people rose against Cromwell, as the type of the New Man about the King. The shouts of 'Cow Crummock' left the Lords in little doubt as to who was marked out to be their Jonas.

At the same time other causes had embittered the feelings of the Court circle against Cromwell. The separation from Rome was already of some six years standing, and the memory of More and Fisher perhaps grown faint; but there had been more recent executions, Exeter and Montagu, Neville, Fortescue, Carew. The peers who had been compelled to carry through the treason trials of their friends and relatives did not forgive a plebeian minister who had arranged them. And in the background there was the great body of the bishops, careful men, some timorous, most diplomatic, all Court-appointed. They knew that Cromwell had an intimate and unfriendly knowledge of their careers. Their innate conservatism and the remains of their pride revolted against this layman who held all the damaging and closely detailed information possessed by a financial go-between. Few of the bishops could rest easy in the presence of the King's Grace's Vicegerent in Spirituals. Still, these hatreds weighed little in the balance as against his successful administration in home affairs, and Cromwell would perhaps have remained invulnerable but for his failing foreign policy.

The years of Cromwell's greatest security covered the period which lay between the death of Anne Boleyn in May 1536 and the close of the King's eligible widowerhood in the first days of 1540. During 1539 the Privy Seal had unwisely allowed himself to become the supporter of a particular royal marriage (with Anne of Cleves) in the development of general foreign policy.

There were various difficulties over the Cleves alliance. In the first place Cromwell lacked that close knowledge of the limited sphere of foreign politics in which Wolsey had worked. He was also, perhaps, too conscious of the dangers which might arise from a Roman Catholic marriage; the possibility that a wedding with the Duchess of Milan, as an example, might in the end eventually bring back the Pope. At the same time, viewed as a counterpoise, the German Lutherans at the time meant very little.

There is also the curious haze that lies over the question of the religion of the Princess of Cleves. In the intricacies of the German princely families it is more than usually difficult to determine the religious affiliations of the princesses of that house. Stress was laid on the admirable upbringing that Anne of Cleves had received from her mother; but there is little doubt that the elder lady remained a Catholic throughout her life. Her confessor had been the well-known writer Dom Joannes Justus Lanspergius, prior of the charterhouse of Our Lady of Compassion at Cantave. It was only at Easter 1543 that her son the Duke agreed to receive the Sacrament under both kinds. There was no doubt that the Elector and Electress of Saxony, the bride's brother-in-law and sister were Lutheran leaders. The Princess Anne herself was at this time quite ready to marry a sovereign, who had broken with the Pope; but it is not surprising that in later life she returned to the Old Religion. Her brother soon returned to the Catholic Church.

It is more customary to query the effect of the Cleves marriage on Cromwell's fall, and it is true that his relentless enemies, especially the Bishop of Winchester, were always waiting. It may perhaps be said that they approached the King when his mind was disturbed by the inadequacies that he found in his new bride. The Duke of Cleves abandoned him politically and he was now moving to discard the Queen.

This was the state of affairs when Cromwell received his last promotion. With the many forces against him it is extraordinary how weak were the supports which he could count on then. Among the great officers of State he had one constant friend, the Archbishop of Canterbury, Cranmer. They were very different in character, poles apart in cast of mind, but agreed on policy. In any case Cranmer had serious disadvantages as an ally in extremity; for he was not ruthless, he became timorous at a crisis, he was sincere about tiresome religious detail. Beyond the Archbishop there was not one among the leaders at the Court whose falsetto expressions of devotion towards the Lord Privy Seal could be held to reflect a true opinion. In the consciously elaborate phraseology of his colleagues' letters one element recurs, an irony, sometimes detached, more often bitter, always present.

Still difficult as was his position, Cromwell was bound to go forward. An organization of dependants and agents had grown up about him, cumbrous and inescapable. Among the younger politicians was Sir Edward Seymour, now Lord Hertford. He had a good will towards the older man as long as he remained in his position. A constant influence on policy made it necessary to be well-informed; there was no question of a quiet withdrawal. Besides in this April it was manifest that the King still needed him. During the period that his services were required, some change in the attitude of the foreign powers could perhaps develop, or his enemies in England might yet play into his hands. For at the moment Cromwell was engaged on the perfecting of an important financial service to the Crown, the carrying through of the suppression of the hospitals of St John of Jerusalem in England, and until these plans were completed he seemed safe.

This suppression indicates something of the general nature of his work in liquidating the religious orders; for it required an experienced technique in manipulating surrenders, in calculating and arranging pensions, and in securing the transfer of the buildings and landed property in good condition. There was also always needed that element of delicate personal negotiation in which the Vicegerent in Spirituals excelled. A not wholly serious correspondence between the English Government and the Grand Master in Malta had been carried on over two years. The fullest value as a political factor had been extracted from the Grand Master's imprisonment of an English knight, and the matter was by now reduced to the question of the minimum figure at which the necessary pensions must be fixed. The Lord Prior of England, Sir William Weston, had proved most amenable to each suggestion of the Government. That in the past had been an advantage; but in consequence he was now unfortunately in a position to press for a substantial sum. Cromwell, however, had private information: he was aware of the Lord Prior's decrepit physical condition. He saw that he could prudently make extensive promises. The negotiations for surrender were eased by the grant of an annual life-pension of £1,000 to the Lord Prior, who signed the necessary documents, and then died on the very day of the dissolution of the Order. The whole of the considerable sum was thus saved for the Treasury. It is only a minor instance, but the last, and in some ways the most typical example of Cromwell's methods.

But such methods, when applied through an unemotional balanced judgement unbiased by any personal sympathy, left Cromwell isolated. Each such successful operation carried through with his cold skill removed him further from the general track. Yet despite the honeyed phrases of insincerity by which he was surrounded it is very rare for any great man to be left completely alone in his own circle. In Cromwell's case he had the support of Sir Thomas Wyatt, the poet and ambassador. He belonged to the younger generation and could not help him; but they were both agreed in a carefree and sceptical approach to all the religious phenomena that flowered about them.

Cromwell was always the New Man, self-made, the servant of the new State which his contemporaries could only understand imperfectly. Around him were grouped the courtiers with their consciousness of good birth and sound connections. They in a sense were all united and, acting in their respective stations, negligently, obsequiously, or furtively made their fortunes in that grave financial scramble which gave its tone to the late Henrican Court. It was true that it was their own class, the courtiers and rich squires, which benefited chiefly by their well-founded speculation, but the Privy Seal received no more gratitude from his clients than any other large-scale financier.

In his great new house, whose gardens pressed against the crowded city dwellings, he went through this business, through the mass of correspondence which the summoning of a fresh Parliament always brought him and the despatches of the envoys and of his agents. The plainness of his dress would only emphasize the ostentatious and costly fittings of his chambers, the 'ball of astronomy' upon its tripod on the Flemish carpet, and the 'great muros or looking-glass of steel gilted'. The cushions on the corner seats were worked with the rose gules which formed a part of the Privy Seal's armorial bearings, and the wall space above was hung with an elaborate tapestry on green and red serge, the history of Susanna. It must have been a luxurious set of rooms, but certainly not homely and probably not reassuring to a man in his crisis. A sense of values was evidenced by the hangings and by the paintings of the inlaid Italian tables, but this was possibly the merchant's flair. The rooms at any rate were overcrowded, and in the midst of this accumulation of predominantly sacred art there moved the *bourgeois* Cromwell household, the young unmarried daughters and the dull son Gregory. It was eleven years since his wife had died and Cromwell had not remarried. A certain frost lay on his relations. This seems partly caused by the fact that his heir was this unhopeful boy.

Save through his son's recent marriage to Elizabeth Seymour, he had no marriage links with the great families. Those who, like Stephen Vaughan, had been his friends were now his servants. He was too 'great' and perhaps his knowledge of private affairs was too intimate for the survival of friendship. Similarly his generosity to his relatives was hardly of a kind to promote intimacy. He settled his relatives in a moderate station and paid the expenses this involved. For instance, there was a bill of some pounds to be met which his sister Mrs Wellyfed had owed to her maltster. He could deal proudly with his dependant clan, but could hardly expect support from them. Like all the *bourgeois* ministers who were in time to serve the monarchies, he stood inevitably in isolation, drawn from his own class by the very intimacy of his State service.

In his earlier years he had made efforts and had taken a faint part in that formal hunting which gave consistency to the routine of the courtier's country life. But he was now grown elderly for such exertion, and he no longer needed proof that the gentry who paid interest on his loans were also prepared to entertain him. His earldom placed him far beyond such questionings. The high title of Essex with its half-royal associations had passed from Mandeville to Bohun and Bourchier: the great chamberlainship also had descended through equally exalted generations.

In May there were charges against Lord Lisle, the Governor of Calais, and his chaplain. They were accused of secret dealings with Cardinal Pole's agents, that same Cardinal who had accused Cromwell of resembling the demoniac among the tombs in the New Testament. This was a final manifestation of one aspect of the White Rose families for Lord Lisle was a natural son of Edward IV and had married the aunt of that child-bride who had brought the Lisle title to Charles Brandon so long ago. Since anti-Roman patriotism was the Privy Seal's strong suit, all rumours of treachery would serve to assist him. It was, however, late to work up this small matter. Cromwell was surely too isolated a man not to be fully conscious of the new set of the tide.

If only he could leave churchmanship behind and concentrate on pure politics he might yet save himself. He had been to Parliament in his new robes, the crimson velvet furred with miniver of his earldom, that symbol of a future security; but a constant straining political effort paid for this magnificence. On April 31 * he was due at a Chapter of the Garter, where it was his duty as Earl of Essex to offer up the banner of the Earl of Shrewsbury, just deceased. This was perhaps his line of safety, if he could have become securely the great lay lord and shake off the religious aspect of his work, the Vicegerency in Spirituals and all that it implied. The monasteries were dissolved and a whole section of his life was finished. For six years he had been dealing with aspiring monks zealous for promotion, and now at last they had been hustled from the scene. But it was his ecclesiastical enemies who still pursued him.

In his great hall the Marquess of Dorset's arms would serve to remind him of his earlier service, the gilded mantecor and the unicorn. But he could not rely on those who were now his fellow-nobles. The Italian pictures hung beside his windows, the Pietà and the painting of the Passion and the Rape of Lucrece; while below, in his strong room, 'the silver plate, crosses, chalices and other spoils of the Church' had been collected. These were hardly reassuring treasures. Spread along the wall in the parlour was the carved woodwork of the King's arms and the Queen's with an eagle and a white greyhound; and on the King all depended.

Bishop Gardiner and the Duke of Norfolk displayed a certain skill in bringing down the Lord Privy Seal. The King was disenchanted. There was something a trifle ludicrous about the whole episode of the Cleves marriage and the attraction that he felt for Catherine Howard, one of the Duke of Norfolk's nieces, who had lately been brought upon the scene suggested a world in which he would have no need of Thomas Cromwell.

As the years passed the Privy Seal became less mobile. In 1536 he had spent nearly a month at Windsor Castle[1] and in the

---

[1] Cf. Cromwell's Itinerary printed in R. B. Merriman, *Life and Letters of Thomas Cromwell* (1900), vol. II.   * Old Style.

following years he had been for a few days with the King at his
royal manors at Woking, Grafton, Ampthill, Mortlake and Oatlands and then at Grafton for a second visit. He had been again at
Oatlands with the King in July 1539; from that month onwards
he seems to have stayed continuously in London except for a short
journey of four days in January to Greenwich Palace. One has the
feeling that he knew his power was ending.

Cromwell was probably a better judge of men of his own background than he was of members of the aristocracy. In any event it
seems strange that he gave any favour to Walter Hungerford. He
had been recommended to him as a young man and had been
appointed sheriff of Wiltshire through his aid and had been raised
to the peerage as Lord Hungerford of Heytesbury on his motion.
The family had had a tarnished past. Lord Hungerford's stepmother a widow had been hanged in 1524 for murdering her first
husband. He himself was noted for his cruelty to his wife, whom he
imprisoned. The scene of both these tragedies was his Wiltshire
home. It is now the smiling, water-surrounded ruin of Farleigh
Castle.

Hungerford's value to the attackers arose from the fact that he
was the Lord Privy Seal's solitary disreputable associate. Also use
could be made of his Lutheran dependants. Attention was concentrated on his friends Robert Barnes and William Jerome, the vicar
of Stepney, his home parish. These were accused of being sacra-
mentaries, that is to say Anabaptists, and burned as such. The
Lord Privy Seal himself was accused of selling export licences,
granting passports and drawing up commissions without the royal
knowledge and of being a heretic and a favourer of the sacra-
mentaries. The King, provided that he believed these charges,
must have felt that his servant indeed had slipped away from
him.

The Duke of Norfolk arrested the Lord Privy Seal as he sat at the
Council Table. Later he was visited in the Tower by the Duke
accompanied by Lord Southampton, who asked him to provide
evidence that the King had stated that he had not consummated
his marriage with Anne of Cleves. He had been arrested on 10 June
and was executed on Tower Hill on 27 July. On the scaffold he
denied with perfect truth that he had ever been a sacramentary

and stated that he died a faithful Catholic as the King understood that term. On the same day Lord Hungerford was beheaded on a conviction for unnatural vice. It was a sad ending and much of the detail seems irrelevant. The key to the situation lay in the fact that the Lord Privy Seal had now become expendable.

PART THREE

THE LAST DECADE

22 Derich Born

23 Derich Berck of Cologne

I

The Steelyard Merchants

It is rare for a sovereign to show gratitude for the removal of a once-trusted minister, but normally such sentiments as may be aroused are submerged by the kaleidoscopic passage of events. In the case of Cromwell's fall King Henry had been left with what he had before, the increasingly battered figure of the Duke of Norfolk and the wise and shuttered visage of the Bishop of Winchester. After a brief episode in which these two politicians were brought vividly before him, the King's last years were spent in gradually disembarrassing himself of both of them. During this final period of King Henry's reign one man made forward, the Earl of Hertford, better known by his later title as the Protector Somerset. It was not an unwise move of Thomas Cromwell when he made a family alliance with the Seymour family.

The immediate effect of the sexual appetite frustrated in the King by Anne of Cleves was the short episode of the marriage and consequently the reign as Queen of Catherine Howard. The first problem is why the Duke and the Bishop of Winchester agreed to bring her forward. The only reasonable explanation seems to be that the Duke was unaware of her personal history and of her character. She was the daughter of Lord Edmund Howard, his spendthrift brother, and had been brought up by her step-grandmother the Dowager Duchess at Horsham St Faith. She seems to have been young; the date of her birth is undiscoverable. No specimen of her handwriting remains but it is possible that she could only write with difficulty. She had learned to play upon the virginals. The Dowager had retained for life the old Howard house in Lambeth and it was there that she was brought and met the King.

M

King Henry was suffering from the strain of his relationship with
Anne of Cleves. He became devoted to and married the Duke of
Norfolk's niece. As far as solid facts are concerned we know almost
nothing about her opinions, her influence or her reign. She has
been built up as a Catholic, but there seems no evidence to support
this. She does not seem in any way to have endeavoured to prevent
the execution of Lady Salisbury. It is possible that the influence of
her step-grandmother and that of those whom she had met at
Horsham may have given her a liking for the Old Religion. We
cannot tell. The Duke can be termed a conservative, but it is
difficult to be more explicit. As for the Bishop of Winchester, he
was a conservative likewise and had certainly some Catholic preferences, but there is no reason to suppose that he was, even
secretly, a Romanist. He seems to have had no interest in the Holy
See and then his outlook was primarily that of a convinced
Erastian.

The Queen's reign lasted only fourteen months,[1] the first period
passed in the palaces round London and the second summer in a
progress to the North to York and Pontefract. She was arrested in
November 1541 soon after the Court returned in the rainy season
to Wolsey's former house at Hampton Court. Most of the information about her that we possess deals with her life at Horsham St
Faith before her marriage and on her relations with Francis Dere-
ham and Thomas Colepepper. It was the Queen's immediate relations who suffered most after her own execution. The Dowager
Duchess and her daughter the Countess of Bridgwater were for a
time in the Tower. The Duke's letter to the King on this occasion
refers to 'my ungracious mother-in-law and my lewd sister of
Bridgewater'. It seems fairly clear that they had deceived him or
perhaps it is more accurate to say that there were some facts which
they knew which would have alerted his experienced mind. Alto-
gether it had been a most unsuccessful operation.

Archbishop Cranmer had precipitated the Queen's death and
the Duke of Norfolk's fall from power and favour. The chief prosecution witnesses against the Queen had come to him and he over-

---

[1] There has been one modern biography of this Queen, Lacey Baldwin Smith, *A
Tudor Tragedy, The Life and Times of Catherine Howard*, published in 1961. This is an
interesting study, as a minor point the author confuses Horsham St Faith in Norfolk
with Horsham in Sussex.

came his timidity and brought the evidence before the King. It seems probable that he was actuated by a deep bitterness against the Duke, who had compassed the death of Thomas Cromwell. For the remainder of the reign the Archbishop of Canterbury remained secure in his predominant position.

During this time Holbein died in his house in the parish of St Andrew Undershaft, one of the victims of a sharp attack of the plague which had come to London. The exact date is not known, but it was some time in the late autumn of 1543.[1] He was working until the last and he left unfinished his big portrait of Henry VIII granting a charter to the Barber Surgeons Company. His executor, who was also in regard to a small sum his creditor, was John of Antwerp, goldsmith. He was one of the merchants of the Steelyard and this seems the point at which to touch on the range of portraits and the other work that Holbein did for this foreign corporation.

It is not surprising that these portraits were not painted in his earlier life. It seems clear that as a group the members wished to engage the services of an established painter. The suggestion[2] that Nicholas Kratzer, the astronomer royal, whom he painted on his first visit to England introduced him at the Steelyard seems very probable. Kratzer himself came from Munich. The Steelyard merchants were the only group among all those of whom he painted individual portraits in England who cannot be considered to be in a broad sense courtiers. Nevertheless, the King was always conscious of the Steelyard and of the services that its members could do for him.

The Steelyard was a truly venerable foreign merchant body and somewhat past its better days. It was the headquarters of the members of the Hanseatic League situated in the City and with access to the river. Its varied goods were all brought in by sea. Through the centuries it had been built into the organization of London and it sent an alderman to the City Council. It was built into the religious complex of the host city. There are no references to a chapel or to a chaplain. The cities of the Hanseatic League had accepted Lutheranism very early. Thus, although the Steelyard bore the double-headed eagle of the Empire, there was no

---

[1] At some date between 7 October and 29 November 1543.
[2] Cf. Arthur B. Chamberlain, *Hans Holbein the Younger* (1913), vol. II, p. 4.

opposition to the religious changes. Their members' interests were strictly mercantile. There was never a time when the Steelyard could be charged with actions in the field of English politics.

The old building stood on the site which was later occupied by the railway station at Cannon Street. The steelyard has long since disappeared and it is not easy to imagine it. The main frontage was on Thames Street and the land behind stretched to the water's edge. It was surrounded by a turreted wall and the entrance had three fortified gateways. Inside there was the old stone guildhall and council chamber set in a garden planted with fruit trees and vines. Beside the main gate there were vaults where Rhenish wine was husbanded and sold. Windgoose Alley ran from Thames Street to the river and gave access to the shops. These were small and had behind them only a bedroom and a sitting-room for the merchant. No women or strangers slept within the Steelyard and its gates were closed each evening at nine o'clock. Holbein has thrown much light upon the life there.

The most elaborate of the Steelyard portraits is that of George Gisze now in the Berlin Museum. He is seen as a young man in the flat black cap, which all the merchants wore. The table at which he sits has a coloured cloth and on this is a Venetian vase filled with carnations. The space seems small for the painted wooden walls are close behind him. On the table are the objects in daily use, a seal, an inkstand, scissors, a leather case with metal bands and clasps and a box containing money. From the shelves behind him hang scales for weighing gold, a seal attached to a long chain and a metal ball for string. There are letters caught upon a rail beside him and on a shelf a heavy book, perhaps accounts. He himself is quiet and self-possessed. Money has come to him. He brings to mind the figures of Basel mercantile patricians in Holbein's youth. His dress is most elaborate, rose-coloured silk with an overcoat of black and a fine white linen shirt. Although there is no reason to suppose that he frequented King Henry's Court, he was the type of guest whom it must have been a pleasure for Thomas Cromwell to entertain.

It is curious that nearly all the portraits of the Steelyard merchants represent young men. This may have been because the arrangements of the London house only made provision for bachelor representatives to England. The only rather older man portrayed was Hermann Hildebrand Wedigh, a member of a family from Cologne, who had had connections with the London Steelyard as far back as 1480. It seems that unlike the North Germans they may have been of Catholic preferences since the headquarters of his family was in the spiritual electorate. But somehow the question of religion never seems to have arisen where the members of the Steelyard were concerned.

All the members of the corporation were represented sitting at their desks and all were wearing the same flat black cap. It has been suggested that these smaller portraits were intended as gifts to be hung permanently in the hall or council chamber. Some of them are painted wearing an overcoat with a deep fur collar often lined with lighter fur. This was the dress in which they would go about their business outside the Steelyard. Three of the portraits date from 1533, those of Derich Born, Derich Tybis and Cyriacus Fallen. They are all young men and the most attractive is the portrait of Derich Born now preserved at Windsor Castle.[1] The last of the series dates from 1536 and is again a portrait of a rather older man Derich Berck, who like the Wedighs was a native of Cologne. This portrait[2] is now at Petworth.

It is an interesting study to consider these portraits as a group. The most sympathetic are those of the younger men. They are all merchants whose fortunes have been inherited; they have never had the wear and tear of effort. Successful trade was all important to them. They would certainly do their best to satisfy that Court under whose protection the Steelyard lay. They would transcribe German letters and send forward correspondence to the King's 'orators in High Almayne'. Seemly decorations would be put up on formal occasions like the 'mountain' designed by Holbein for the coronation of Queen Anne Boleyn whose procession passed through Thames Street. A fountain of Helicon in white marble played Rhenish wine continually. Among the figures at the base was that of Calliope. The merchants of the Steelyard were drawn up in the gateway to welcome, as she passed, their second Queen. One has the sense that in these turbid years trade was their master.

---

[1] For the reproduction of the portrait of Derich Born see p. 176.
[2] For the reproduction of the portrait of Derich Berck see p. 177.

It is curious that apart from the pictures painted in the very early period of his years with Thomas More, riches was the note that marked the great majority of the subjects of the Holbein portraits. These riches were either easily come by or in the case of the English courtiers the fruit of effort. As far as one can discern Holbein seems to have shown in his work a great fidelity. One wonders what was his own attitude towards these matters. All that we know is that he himself did not attain to riches or even to a competence. His wife and his grown-up family abroad in Basel were suitably provided for, but his London situation was rather different. His wife survived him for six years, dying in 1549. Her will describes the effects that he left behind him at Basel on his last visit there in 1538. There was a valise which contained a black cap, a a doublet of smoke-coloured Florentine taffeta and other doublets of black satin, crimson silk and black damask.[1] What he left in London was more disconcerting. By his will he directed that all his goods and his horse be sold and his debts paid. He also left 'for my two childer which be at nurse' the monthly sum of ten shillings and six pence. It has been reasonably suggested[2] that the children's mother died of the same pestilence shortly before Holbein himself. He also left certain debts. He was working until the end for he left his portraits of the Barber Surgeons still unfinished.

[1] The will is printed in Chamberlain, *op. cit.*, II, p. 300.
[2] By Chamberlain, *ibid.*, II, p. 297.

II

The Royal Palaces

The King was only fifty years of age, but his health was breaking; he was often in pain and sometimes comatose; his life was static. The King's elder contemporaries were dying, Southampton in 1542 and the Duke of Suffolk three years later, from among his intimates. Those who had been associated with the White Rose stocks had passed away. Lord Huntingdon, who had arranged the last Pole marriage, died in 1545. Roland Lee, Bishop of Lichfield and Coventry and President of the Council of the Marches, had died in January 1543, and Sir Thomas Wyatt at Sherborne on a journey in the previous October. Both men had lost their influence with Cromwell dead.

Edward Lee, Archbishop of York, died in his palace in the early autumn of 1543. He was fortunate in his hour of going. He had always before his mind the disgraceful and painful end, as he conceived it, of Bishop Fisher. Shortly afterwards both Dr Layton and Dr Legh, the chief among the visitors of the monasteries died. They had worn themselves out with riding hard in Cromwell's service.

It was a strange time for this was the period of the secret victory of the Neo-Protestants. The Earl of Hertford held to this position as did the King's last wife, Catherine Parr, the widowed Lady Latimer, whom he married in 1543. The Duchess of Suffolk, and others of high rank, became a Protestant. This was parallel to the conversions to Calvinism in the same years at the Court of France. The long-established Protestant element in London was growing stronger. The final period of King Henry's reign was in fact suffused by a new Protestant influence of which the sovereign probably was hardly conscious. It was the dawn before the breaking of the Edwardian Reformation, the preparing of the way for

Somerset's regency for the young Prince. The Bishop of Winchester could foresee the future. The Duke of Norfolk was away at Kenninghall. Their day was over.

In these last years of the reign, the King's life was mainly concentrated on his two new palaces Whitehall and Nonsuch. One has the sense that for King Henry the palaces were just the backcloth for his active life. Both his principal buildings have now disappeared, Whitehall which arose upon the site of Wolsey's town house of York Place and the new works at Nonsuch. The first palace was to have been completed for Anne Boleyn; but the great painting of the King and his parents features his third Queen, Jane Seymour. The suggestion[1] by Roy Strong that Holbein's great work was originally placed around a window and on the upper levels of the wall of the Whitehall privy chamber appears convincing. Beneath the window would have stood the royal throne. Dr Strong also draws attention to the use of gold, a note which may be said to recur throughout King Henry's reign. 'It is undeniable,' he writes,[2] 'that in spite of all the splendour of the ceilings and carved woodwork, the ultimate *coup de théâtre* was achieved through movables and everything was but a variation on a single theme, gold. The ceilings were gold, the panelling was picked out in gold, gold thread ran through the tapestries, the fabric hangings and upholstery were gold or shot with gold, the utensils were almost all gold or silver gilt and everywhere and on everything there were massive heavy gold embroidery and fringing.' The stone gallery at Whitehall dates from these years. It is curious that the new buildings contained the gallery from Wolsey's house at Esher, which was re-erected there. All accounts agree that Whitehall in King Henry's time was not externally impressive. On one side lay the river and to the southward there still extended the ancient orchards.

One aspect of the palace was quite novel. This was the decoration of the gates which were put up to enable traffic to pass from Westminster to the City across the extensive royal estate. The so-called Holbein Gate was of chequered flint and brickwork with the King's arms over the archway and the Tudor rose and port-

---

[1] Made by Roy Strong in *Holbein and Henry VIII* (1967), pp. 50–3.
[2] *ibid.*, p. 24.

cullis badges, but it also had four terracotta roundels of Roman
Emperors set into the wall surface. The King Street gate derived
directly from French models. There were antique busts and two
towers with onion domes. One cannot tell whether these features
pleased contemporaries.

The last years of the reign were employed in the building of
Nonsuch Palace. This was begun in April 1538 and was still unfinished at the King's death. It is clear that the construction was in
part influenced by the château of Chambord, which was still
building, and by the gallery at Fontainebleau. The architect
Niccolo de Modena had come direct from the French Court.[1] To
obtain a perfect site the old village and church of Cuddington
were swept away. The materials used in the new palace were in
part old-fashioned. The inner court, which was approached from
the outer court through a gatehouse and up a flight of steps, had a
lower part of stone and upper part of half-timber work; but the
most characteristic part of the building was the block forming the
far side of the inner court and facing outwards on to the gardens.
The block consisted of a long range of buildings between two very
large octagonal towers whose upper parts developed into many-
windowed pavilions crowned by pointed lead roofs and pinnacled
with vanes. These last were characteristic of earlier English building, as in Henry VII's palace at Richmond.

Hundreds of feet of wall space were encrusted with plasterwork
panels in high relief, while the gateway into the inner courtyard
was crowned with statues of the Roman Emperors. The privy
chamber at Nonsuch had a costly fountain in the form of a silver
serpent under the foot of a lion, apparently derived from the alabaster fountain in the privy chamber of Whitehall. One gains the
impression that the King was not deeply concerned with all these
details. He was content to pour out his moneys with a single motive
to surpass the works that the King of France was now engaged on.
His personal taste hardly seems to have entered into such a matter.
He was very simply concerned to outdo Francis I in glory.

---

[1] For the account of Nonsuch cf. Strong, *Holbein and Henry VIII*, pp. 10, 66 and 71;
and J. Summerson, *Architecture in Britain* (1953).

III

The Naval Service

The quality of the foreign policy of the reign changed as the King grew older. In his first years of rule there was an element almost of masquerade, which is seen reflected in the Field of the Cloth of Gold. The policy of Cardinal Wolsey was always serious with a strong tendency to sympathize with the old French monarchy. It was only the King himself who would allow an element of personal rivalry to confuse the issue. In those early days the strange figure of the Emperor Maximilian introduced an element of unreality as a consequence of his readiness to hire his services for a money payment. In the central period of the reign there was a strong motive for maintaining the peace for this best accorded with the domestic policy of Thomas Cromwell. Peace with the greater foreign powers, or from abroad, was necessary for those halcyon years in which the peers and landed gentry regurgitated that England-wide possession the many acres of monastic land.

Curiously enough the last years of the reign were marked by a more active foreign policy carried through against Scotland and the King of France. But this policy was hardly in any direct sense King Henry's work. The ulcer on his thigh, which had plagued him for several years, was now in a serious condition. Even though the motive for the building of Nonsuch Palace was the determination to surpass King Francis, Henry VIII had left behind him that acute sense of personal rivalry with European sovereigns, with King Francis and with the Emperor Charles V. All three were ageing. The King of France in these last years was bound within the life of his own Court, now lit by the engaging personalities of his own and his son's mistresses, the Duchess of Etampes and the Duchess of Valentinois. King Francis at this time was very kind to his daughter-in-law Catherine de Medicis. One has the sense that England was far away from his preoccupations.

It was the same with the Emperor in his own fashion. Once his aunt Catherine of Aragon was dead and the Lady Mary had, on his advice, made her peace with her father, there was little concern for England save for those commercial relations in which the ruler of the Low Countries must be involved. The key point in the English situation was that King Henry had an undoubted heir, his only son.

On the domestic side King Henry's health had its effect. He now lacked that interest in youth, which is the characteristic outlook of the vain man whose middle-aged body has at length betrayed him. All those who had reached their influence in 1540 remained around their sovereign until the end, all save the Earl of Surrey. No new men joined them. The idea of a fresh youthful generation had lost its charms for their pain-racked sovereign.

From one angle it may seem that there was a *continuum* from 1546 until the death of Edward VI in 1553. The Privy Council had now gained its importance:[1] the King was surrounded by his ministers who had long weathered in the royal service. The two active leaders were now the Earl of Hertford and Lord Lisle, who would divide the next reign between them as the Protector Somerset and the Duke of Northumberland. And one here comes across for the first time that note of efficiency and in particular military efficiency, which would always mark Lord Lisle's great reputation.

Very few of the courtiers, except those who came up through the Law, could be really considered as 'new men' and Lord Lisle had been at Court since his beginning. He was the elder son of Edmund Dudley, the Councillor to Henry VII, who had been executed in the first year of the present reign for his extortions. The boy had been restored in blood when ten years old in 1512 and had been given over to the guardianship of Sir Edward Guildford,[2] Marshal of Calais, who had given him in marriage to his only child. Her mother was a sister of old Lord Delawarr and her father

---

[1] Cf. J. J. Scarisbrick *Henry VIII*, (1968), p. 426.
[2] The name is spelt Guildford or Guldeford. It re-appears in Northumberland's younger son, the husband of Lady Jane Grey, Lord Guildford Dudley.

was the head of one line of a great family of the South Country squirearchy, prudent and conservative. She made a self-effacing and prolific wife to him; but in the end the Duchess of Northumberland died as a Catholic in Queen Mary's reign.

The Lisle peerage, which came to him through his mother, brought him some descents from the high fifteenth-century families. He was before all else a soldier with some resemblance to the bold *condottieri* in fifteenth-century Italy. Like them he had great courage. He was seduced, as many of them also were, by the desire for riches. There was nothing that he would not venture; but he could not plan. All this, however, lay in the future.

Now in 1543 his service hitherto was mainly military. Sir John Dudley had been knighted in 1523, the year that he came of age, when serving as Lieutenant of the Spears at Calais. In 1534 he received the relatively subordinate office of Master of the Armoury in the Tower; he held one diplomatic appointment and a seat in Parliament. In 1537 he became Vice-Admiral of England. He was one of those men of middle rank whom the fall of the Howards would bring forward. In the late autumn of 1542 he was made Warden of the Scottish Marches and in the following January he was appointed Lord High Admiral, a great office that he held for the remainder of the reign.

This was the period in which the fortresses were built to guard the south-eastern coast against the French. The one perfect survivor is Deal Castle. It is in a modern sense a careful fortification; the Middle Ages have been left behind. It is low and squat standing upon the sea, with a single outer bastion and within this six rounded parapets shaped like half moons: these all contained embrasures for the guns. The building throughout was local stone. Deal Castle was quite novel like the military architecture that was developing in Italy; it would remain a virgin fortress. The great works built at Berwick-on-Tweed about this time reflect the same ideas.

The organization found in the Elizabethan naval service has its origin in this period. The Navy Board, for instance, dates from a patent signed on 22 April 1546.[1] There was a Lieutenant of the Navy, a Treasurer of Marine Causes, a Comptroller, a Sur-

[1] Cf. *The Royal Navy, a History*, ed. William Laird Clowes, vol. I, pp. 437–8.

veyor of Ships and a Master of the Ordnance of the Navy. There was also the long-established office of the Clerk of the Ships.

There was now a certain element of exchange between commands at sea and these shore appointments. Thus Sir William Woodhouse became Master of the Ordnance after commanding the *Jesus of Lubeck* in the Narrow Seas. Several other courtiers had gone on board to carry out the King's service on the sea.[1] Thus in addition to the Lord High Admiral there were Lord William Howard in the *Great Venice* and Lord Clinton in the *Lesse Gallienne*. Both would fill that high office in time. Lord William, whom the King had always liked, had had some difficulties at the time of the fall of his niece Queen Catherine.[2] There was also Sir Richard Wingfield in the *Marian* and Sir John Clere in the *Sweepstake*. Sir Thomas Clere was Lieutenant of the Admiralty. Other captains had a different background and perhaps their appointments were more permanent. Thus on 4 April 1546 Lord Lisle wrote to the Council,[3] 'Out of the Narrow Seas on the 20th ult. we sent the Marie Fortune of London, 120 tons, captain, Thomas Ranger, yeoman of the Guard.'

One document throws a certain light on the recruitment of the naval service. It is a survey of strangers lodging in two districts of London,[4] East Smithfield and St Katharine's lane with the Mercate Place adjoining. It therefore deals with men of a certain substance. Native Londoners are not included, nor are the vagrant poor. The master gunner of a naval vessel was the equivalent of a petty, or more exactly of a warrant, officer. These men were probably engaged for the duration of a ship's commission.

At the date of the survey Richard Haynes, master gunner, with Thomas Wilde, master gunner's mate, and John Grimsbye, gunner members of the ships company of the *Rose Lyon* were all lodging at Thomas Harry's house 'tarrying the setting forth of the same ship'. Conrad Blainkeston, 36, a gunner out of wages that is to say without employment, is described as born in High 'Douchelande'; he

---

[1] *Letter and Papers, Henry VIII*, 1546, p. 234.
[2] Lord William Howard, later first Lord Howard of Effingham was a contemporary of his step-niece. He was deprived of the manor of Tottenham after her fall.
[3] *Letters and Papers, Henry VIII*, 1546, p. 265.
[4] *Letters and Papers, Henry VIII*, 1545, pp. 65–6.

had lodged since Saturday was seven night with Thomas Lee and had served for the last fifteen months first in the *New Barke* and then in the *Rose Lyon*. John Thomson, a gunner born at Lincoln was at Creekes' waiting to serve where he shall be appointed. He, likewise, had served last year in the *New Barke* and the *Rose Lyon*. In the same house there also lodged Anthony Leache, 40, a purser born in Lincolnshire, who had been for five months in the *Great John Evangelist*. These six men may, perhaps, be grouped together.

The next two names possibly refer to merchant seamen, although the reference in each case to their readiness to serve where appointed suggests the naval service. John Barne, a gunner, born in Norwich and now lodging at Cressewelle's house had been borne, till yesterday in the *Christopher Constable*. Geoffrey Symson, carpenter, born in Norfolk, 30, tall, living in John Watson's house had served last winter in the *Jesus of Callais*. In these instances it is the two ships' names which suggest the merchant service. The case of Andrew Britowe is, however, clear. He is described as 24, tall and unmarried, born in the Isle of Wight and lodging for four days at Thomas Hall's. He had come from Wight to go with Collyns, one of the King's gunners.

A more detailed examination of this list gives some further details of the setting. James Browne, master of the *Mary Awdreys*, a merchantman, had been lying for ten days very sick in Walter Bervalles' house. Henry Varioroke and Godfrey Vancombe, 26, Dutchmen, had lodged with Mr Miter, tailor, in Black Chapel Town for a quarter of a year. Anthony Menill, 60, born in Yorkshire, had stayed since Martinmass at the sign of 'The Three Nuns' without Aldgate, abiding there for 'counsell of the Lawe'. Robert Fillippses, tall, 25, labourer, had been for three weeks in Creekes's house. He had served as tiler for 6d a day at My Lady Lewis's house at Hogges Dunne (Hoxton?). His last abode was with Mr Wharton, comptroller of My Lord of Norfolk's household, who dismissed him for his light condition. Nicholas Coyner, Dutchman, shoemaker, lodging at Anne Roger's house, repaired out of the West Country at Hamble to procure passage to his own country. Hans Adhaus a Fleming, 20, lodged at Cornelis Mighelle's house and was seeking employment as a castor of guns. James Peter, a man of fifty from the same country lodged in the same house about the sale of merchandise which he bringeth. The foreign names seem usually misspelt. They did not matter.

At the other end of the social scale the officers had gone aboard the royal ships that were lying in Portsmouth Harbour. The King was in the *Henry Grace à Dieu*, which wore the flag of the Lord High Admiral. On leaving the anchorage one of the larger vessels, the *Mary Rose*, which had been re-built in 1526 and was now commanded by Sir Peter Carew, turned turtle and sank in the fair way. It seems to have been smooth weather towards the end of July 1546, but the open lower ports were only sixteen inches above the water's edge and the sea came in when the helm was put hard over.[1]

In many ways in spite of the French war, which sometimes was pursued just languidly, the general situation seemed quite normal. For instance a Spaniard was engaged as an officer in the royal service.[2] On 13 April 1546 there was a warrant issued from the Privy Council for £20 for one Madriachaga, a Spaniard retained since Christmas to have been captain of the *Galley Subtil*.

It is interesting that nothing prevented the import of alum in Spanish bottoms. This was derived from the alum mine on the slopes of the Tolfa hills in the States of the Church. By a bargain made between Stephen Vaughan, who had been Cromwell's factor, and two Spanish merchants resident at Antwerp this Roman alum was to be shipped from Civita Vecchia to Cadiz and then reshipped and landed at Southampton. It was the only mineral of commercial value in the papal territory. In these years there was nothing in restraint of trade.

[1] This is discussed in Laird Clowes, *op. cit.* vol. I, p. 463.
[2] Cf. for these two examples, *Letters and Papers, Henry VIII*, 1546, part I, p. 289 and p. 171.

IV

The Earl of Surrey

The Earl of Surrey[1] was the youngest of all those courtiers who played a considerable part in King Henry's reign. The date of his birth is described approximately as 1517 and he was the Duke of Norfolk's eldest son. He had had a difficult childhood caught between his mother and his father's mistress and disliked by both of them. There was in those days no warmth towards him from his own father.

The King had been conscious of him early, for at the age of ten he had been brought to Windsor to be educated with the Duke of Richmond, who was later married to his only sister. Lord Surrey was not a young man whom the King could like. He was proud and amorous and self-sufficient; he could never give the King his meed of praise. Any office or gift that he received from the royal bounty was what his sovereign could not refuse to Norfolk's heir.

His marriage had naturally exercised his father. At first he had thought of the Marney heiress and then the idea had come to him that the King might agree to give to him the Lady Mary, who had been bastardized; but Anne Boleyn had put an end to this. It would not be prudent to build up her stepdaughter in any way. Anne Boleyn was Marchioness of Pembroke at this time and her alliance with the Duke was still intact. Lord Surrey was then married in 1532 to Lady Frances Vere the youngest daughter of the fifteenth Earl of Oxford. They were both fifteen. The bride was unfortunately penniless. She had nothing to recommend her except her placid temperament and her great descent.

Surrey had pleased the French Court on his youthful visits, but it seems that he had no ideas on politics. As to religion his sister said

Cf. the drawing by Holbein facing p. 193.

Southwell Knight.

ETTATIS SV 3

24 Sir Richard Southwell

ho: Earle of Surry.

25 Henry Howard, Earl of Surrey

at his trial that he favoured the old worship; there is no other evidence.

The King gave him the Garter in 1541. He certainly showed no interest in acquiring monastic land. He built a house for himself, which has long since disappeared, just outside Norwich. This he called Mount Surrey. He was wildly extravagant and as can be seen by his dealings with his manors in East Anglia, land ran through his fingers. He had on two occasions, the first when he was only nineteen, attended at both the executions of his cousins, who had been Queens. This was the sort of thing that he must do to extricate his House from their misfortunes.

For the last seven years of his life he and Norfolk had what is best called a working partnership. There was no real closeness, his father could not control him. For example, as the Duke with his old tired wisdom looked out across the waste of waters there appeared to him to be a single remedy. Somehow he must forge a marriage alliance with the Seymours. His daughter the Duchess of Richmond was at home with him, ageing as far as the marriage market was concerned, a virgin widow. She was very plain and had lately taken up with the new Religion. It was she who at a later date would establish Foxe, the author of *The Book of Martyrs*, within the home life of the Howard family. The Duke thought that he would marry her to Sir Thomas Seymour, Lord Hertford's brother; but Surrey would not agree and still less would he consent that one of his little daughters should be betrothed to Hertford's son. He had an impracticable view about the grandeur of his family which came to him with the Stafford blood.

This had, perhaps, something to do with the fact that he was in a sense solitary.[1] He does not seem to have had friends among his equals. His companions were the young men of those families of the East Anglian gentry who were dependents of his noble stock. It is characteristic of his period that there are very few surviving letters. For the public events of the last years of Surrey's life we have the mass of the State Papers of King Henry's reign. This is the point at which to consider his work as a poet.

---

[1] Cf. the drawing by Holbein facing p. 193. There is also a portrait by Guillim Scrots painted in 1546 the year before Surrey's death. It has always seemed to me that he was to some extent the prototype of 'The Young Man in Red' painted in about 1550 and now at Hampton Court.

The first detailed publication of his poems did not take place till Tottel's Miscellany was issued in 1557. His influence therefore was in the Elizabethan world not the Henrican. The same applies to the work of Sir Thomas Wyatt, whose political career has already been considered. But Surrey had escaped to a much greater degree than Wyatt from the literary influences of the past. He was in many ways a clear precursor.

Wyatt was some fourteen years Lord Surrey's senior, with his various Howard connections, he was of course always aware of the Earl of Surrey, but there seems to be little evidence of any direct contact between them except in 1540–2, the two last years of Wyatt's life. Surrey's *An Excellent Epitaphe of Sir Thomas Wyatt* was apparently written shortly after Wyatt's death.

It is worth noting that Petrarch's sonnet no. cxl is the only one of which both Wyatt and Surrey have left us a translation, or to speak more exactly a modern version. It seems to me the effect of their remoteness from the medieval world of the fourteenth century that causes both Wyatt and Surrey to avoid in their versions any reflection of the transcendental character of Petrarch's feeling for Laura. By the sixteenth century the approach was much more mundane.

Surrey was, at least as far as he is represented in his verse, a true Court poet, a townsman with a deep range of literary reference. There are two aspects of Wyatt's work which find no reflection in the Earl of Surrey's. The first is that detailed comment on the countryside, in Wyatt's case the fields of Kent, that appears in the following familiar lines.[1]

> '*My mothers maydes when they did sowe and Spynne*
> *They sang sometyme a song of the field mowse*
> *That forbycause her livelod was but thinne*
> *Would nedes goe seke her townish systers house.*'

The second is found in a poem written on one of his embassies which has in its subject rather than its style a foretaste of the Elizabethans.[2]

---

[1] Poem, no. 197, lines 1–4. Cf. P. Thomson, *Wyatt*, p. 259.
[2] Poem, no. 97. Cf. *ibid.*, p. 66. Both are printed in *Tottel's Miscellany* (1929), vol. I, ed. Hyder Edward Rollins, p. 82 and p. 81.

> '*Tagus, farewell, that westward with thye stremes*
> *Turns up the graines of gold already tried,*
> *For I with spurre and saile go seke the temmes,*
> *Gaineward the sunne that sheweth her welthy pride.*'

The Earl of Surrey has left us a remarkably consistent body of verse. It consists for the most part of the poetry of love and one can well understand how it evoked the enthusiasm of Sir Philip Sidney. It seems best to begin by quoting the translation of the forty-seventh Epigram of the tenth book of Martial. The first eight lines will serve to show his central position in the development of English poetry.[1]

> '*Martiall, the thinges that do attayn*
> *The happy life, be these, I finde.*
> *The richessee left, not got with pain:*
> *The frutefull ground: the quiet Mynde:*
> *The equal Frend, no grudge, no stryfe:*
> *No charge of rule, nor governance:*
> *Without disease the healthfull lyfe:*
> *The household of continuance.*'

This seems to get the note of his achievement. There is too, the question of Surrey's relations with the 'Fair Geraldine', whose name has attached itself like a burr to his reputation. In fact she was only a little girl, when they were at Court together. Almost nothing is known of her save the bare bones of her life. She was apparently an appealing child, the dowerless niece of the Marquess of Dorset. Her father the ninth Earl of Kildare had died in the Tower of London in 1534 and her mother was living at Beaumanoir in Leicestershire: she and her daughters were dependent on King Henry's bounty. Lady Elizabeth Fitzgerald was apparently a maid of honour in the Lady Mary's household. In 1536 she was a girl of ten, when she attracted Surrey's attention. Seven years later she accepted the hand of Sir Anthony Browne, the veteran courtier. After his death she married Lord Clinton and

---

[1] These are printed under the heading 'The meanes to attain happy life' in *Tottel's Miscellany*, i, p. 26.

died in 1590 as his widow and Countess of Lincoln. She left a detailed and elaborate will, characteristic of the period. In all her
doings she remains a shadow.

It is worth noting that the 'Description and praise of his love
Geraldine'[1] is in fact purely fantasy. Surrey adverts from time to
time to his own childhood.[2]

> *'As proude Windsore where I ain lust and joye,*
> *Witha Kinges sonne my childish yeres did passe*
> *In greater feast than Priam's sonnes at Troy.'*

Some words reflect the spirit of the time quite accurately:[3]

> *'And thereto hath a trothe as just,*
> *As had Penelope the fayre.'*

As one reads through the verse it soon appears that all the life
therein reflected was very far removed from the ideas of the Duke
of Norfolk with his old tired wisdom. There was no cunning in the
young heir's character. It was not that they did not both desire the
glory of their great house: it was rather that the youthful peer
could never see his enemies. He was unhappily blinded by arro-
gance. He was living in an unreal world surrounded by his own
dependents. Surrey would have affrays. He would break the
windows of the citizens when he moved into the town with his
companions, aflame with wine.[4] In consequence he spent some
months in prison. This can be seen as the other side of his private
life which contrasted with the contemplative character of his love
poetry. It seems doubtful whether Bishop Gardiner, his father's
one ally could have helped him: but in any case he was now abroad
negotiating with the Emperor for the English Government.

In a way there was something Elizabethan in Surrey's attitude,
but Sir Philip Sidney for example had the anonymity which safe-
guarded a young man of good position. In the last years of King
Henry the great families were in a state of unstable equilibrium.
In conclusion I will quote some lines from 'A complaint by night

---

[1] *Tottel's Miscellany*, I, p. 9.   [2] *Tottel's Miscellany*, I, p. 12.
[3] *ibid.*, I, p. 19.   [4] Cf. *Letters and Papers, Henry VIII.*

of the lover not beloved.'¹ They give an almost painful impression
of how far removed Surrey stood from coming danger.

> '*The beastes, the ayre, the birdes their song doe cease:*
> *The nightes chare the starres about dothe bring:*
> *Calme is the sea, the waves worke lesse and lesse.*'

¹ *Tottel's Miscellany*, I, p. 10.

V

The Final Years

It is possible that during the final period of the reign the strife
between the parties might seem muted. Ever since Thomas Cromwell's death the power of the Privy Council had revived and it was
inevitable that the greater rivals would find their place at the
Council Board. The King in these years threw himself with vio-
lence into his conflict with the King of France. The struggle with
Scotland, both before the death of James V and in the first years
of the regency for the infant Queen, was secondary to the sovereign's absorption in his French battles. This was *his* war and it was
not a conflict in which any of his ministers was lukewarm; there
was no French party at the English Court.

The Duke of Suffolk soon disappeared and the leading com-
manders were Lord Lisle, who was in charge of the sea forces, and
the old Duke of Norfolk and Lord Hertford, who had the most
pretensions to command on land. In 1544 the King had con-
quered the town and the greater part of the county of Boulogne.
It was a difficult position; his energy was feverish and his strength
was failing.

In the first year the Duke of Norfolk had command in France
and in the succeeding spring his son the Earl of Surrey took his
place. In January 1546 a small defeat of the English forces at St
Etienne by a French column advancing from Montreuil was quite
rightly reported back to England and this resulted in Surrey's
supersession by the Earl of Hertford. At this time Lisle was working upon Hertford's side. The way was opened for the final tragedy.

Many of the State Trials of this reign are confusing, but there
are none in which the origins and courses seem so uncertain as
those which brought about the near-destruction of the House of

Howard. One of the few substantial documents in this case is the account of the first examination of the Duke of Norfolk after he and Lord Surrey had been arrested on 12 December 1546. This took place in the Tower of London in the presence of the Lord Great Chamberlain and the Secretary of State. The Secretary was Sir William Paget, then a figure of relatively small importance, who was at this time merely the echo of the Lord Great Chamberlain – he was of crucial significance, the King's brother-in-law, the Earl of Hertford.

Reading through the document one gets the sense that the Duke was quite bewildered. He had been long in politics: he could not be certain that he could save Lord Surrey; his first duty was to save himself. It was the theory in the sixteenth century that to over-praise a man was quite impossible. He set to work to put a gloss upon the marriage plans that he wished to make with the Seymour family. 'On Tuesday in Whitsun week,' he began,[1] 'I begged the King's help for a marriage between my daughter and Sir Thomas Seymour, and whereas my son of Surrey hath divers daughters, that a cross-marriage might be made between my Lord Great Chamberlain and them, and also whereas my son Thomas hath a son who shall,[2] by his mother, spend two thousand marks a year that he might in later life be married to one of my said Lord's daughters.'

And then he went back to describe his pains and services. He denied that he had ever used a private cypher, and to the question as to the possibility that the Bishop of Rome might break the peace now made between the King's Majesty, the Emperor and the French King he became vehement. 'As God help me and at my most need,' declared the Duke, 'I cannot remember hearing any man speak like words, and as for the Bishop of Rome if I had twenty lives I would rather have spent them all than that he should have any power in this realm, for no man knows better than I through reading history how his usurped power hath increased.

'My Lords, I trust ye think Cromwell's service and mine hath not been like, and yet it is my desire to have no more favour shown for me than was shown to him. He was a false man and surely I am

---

[1] *Letters and Papers, Henry VIII*, vol. 21, part II, 1546, no. 554, pp. 252–3.
[2] Henry later second Viscount Howard of Bindon, born 1542.

a true poor gentleman, I think that since great causes have been
laid to my charge or else I had not been sent hither [to be inter-
rogated in the Tower of London] and I beg that my accursers and
I may be brought face to face, for I will hide nothing. Never gold
was tried better with fire and water than I have been.'

He then settled down to give in rather a pell-mell fashion the
story of his life. 'No man had greater enemies about my sovereign
lord than I have had.' He paused and then continued. 'When I
write that I have had great enemies, the Cardinal confessed to me
at Esher that he had gone about fourteen years to destroy me, by
the setting on of my Lord of Suffolk, the Marquis of Exeter and
My Lord Sandes, who said unless he put me out of the way I
should undo him. Cromwell, when the Marquis of Exeter suffered,
examined his wife more straitly of me than of all other men, as she
sent me word by her brother the Lord Mountjoy. He often said to
me, "My Lord, you are so happy a man that your wife knoweth no
hurt by you, for if she did she would undo you." '

Leaving his wife, he then adverted to his late father-in-law the
Duke of Buckingham, who 'confessed at the bar, my father acting
as [his] judge that of all men living he hated me most. . . . Rhys,
who had married my syster, expressed the same and wished that he
had found means to thrust his dagger in me. The malice borne me
by both my nieces, whom it pleased the King to marry is not
unknown to you. . . . Who tried out the followers of the Lord
Darcy, Sir Robert Constable, Sir John Bulmer, Aske and many
others but only I? Who showed His Majesty the words of my
mother-in-law [in reality stepmother] for which she was attainted
of misprision but I.'

It is worth noting that he accused no living person. It appeared
that all his enemies were justly dead. Sir Rhys ap Gruffydd had
been executed for treason in 1531 and the Dowager Duchess had
died in 1545, the previous year. And then he came to his perora-
tion. 'I have always shown myself a true man to my sovereign, and
have received no profits of His Highness' throne before. Poor man
as I am yet I am his son, his near kinsman. For whose sake should
I be untrue to him?'

When one rereads these rather tangled sentences one gains the
strong impression that the Duke did not know what had now

struck him. He summoned to his aid that fact of his exalted blood, which he so seldom mentioned. He knew that Hertford was a gentle Protestant and that he was fully aware of each distinction in that graded Court. The idea that the Duke had asked the King to persuade the Lord Great Chamberlain to accept in marriage not only his Protestant daughter, but the whole posse of his little grandchildren must have been sweet to him. And then the Duke disclaimed sympathy for the Pope and gave a rather fanciful account of his many enemies. It was true that he had gained nothing but misfortune from the royal marriages of his two nieces. Finally he called in aid his greatest service, the execution of the leaders of the Pilgrimage of Grace.

When this outpouring was finished, the Duke fell silent. He had saved himself. He went back to his quarters in the Tower and stayed there in quietness year after year. He could do nothing to save his son; it had required the whole of his energy to save himself.

Our knowledge of the process against the Earl of Surrey is almost the reverse of that which we possess in the case against his father. Where the Duke of Norfolk is concerned we have a substantial document which he produced in his defence. For Surrey we have certain evidence produced against him and an imperfect complicated series of the charges made by the Crown's advisers. This was an attempt to prove, by the Earl's unguarded words and by the armorial bearings that he set up, that the Government should pass on the King's death to the Duke his father.

The question of the armorial bearings seems very complex. At that date there were among the English noble families a certain number who were entitled through the marriages of heiresses or co-heiresses in former centuries to quarter undifferenced the royal arms of England. Lord Surrey was accused of displaying at Kenninghall the arms of Edward the Confessor, which it was alleged had been granted to the first Mowbray Duke of Norfolk by Richard II. It was admitted that as the representatives of the only daughter of Thomas of Brotherton, the youngest son of Edward I, all the Dukes of Norfolk, first of the Mowbray and then of the Howard line, were entitled to quarter the royal arms. It was asserted, but apparently not proved, that the arms of Edward the

Confessor were from time to time used by the heir to the throne. It was further stated that Garter king at arms had refused permission to Lord Surrey to use this coat.

One wonders what exactly did occur. Two ladies were brought down from Kenninghall, the Duchess of Richmond and Mistress Holland. Both of them wished to spare the Duke, but also to accuse his eldest son. The Duchess in particular was acrimonious against her brother. She drew attention in a somewhat confused statement to his new arms. An examination of the Howard tombs at Thetford in order to find fresh evidence was unsuccessful.[1] Attention was drawn to 'the figure of a little gentlewoman', which stood beneath the full arms of England and France with five labels: but these were presumably the bearings of the Lady Anne, the first wife of the Duke, who bore these legally as the daughter of King Edward.

Two statements contain the core of the accusation against Lord Surrey. Mr Edward Rogers told Sir Gawen Carew that the Earl had said,[2] 'If God should call the King's Majesty unto his mercy (whose life and health the Lord long preserve) he thought no man so meet to have the governance of the Prince, as my Lord his father.' Beside this was placed the words of Master Devereux to Sir Edward Warner.[3] 'Would that he [my Lord Surrey] were accused to the King [for his statement]: if God should call the King to his mercy, who so meet to govern the Prince as my Lord his father.' It seems that these words were fatal to him as a prognostication of the future.

There is no evidence that he thought at all how the Duke of Norfolk might attain to power. Surrey was not a politician. He lived alone in his own world. He was accused of high treason under the act for determining the succession to the throne (Henry VIII, c. vii. sect. 12). He was found guilty and eight days later was beheaded on Tower Hill on 21 January 1547. The King was dying.

---

[1] *Letters and Papers, Henry VIII*, vol. 21, part II, 1546, p. 288.
[2] *ibid.*, p. 246, no. 555, 5.
[3] *ibid.*, p. 244, no. 555, 2.

VI

The King's Death

The King lay dying in the winter weather in St James's Palace at Westminster. It has been suggested that in his later years he inclined towards certain Protestant measures, but I think that the bulk of the evidence suggests that he died as he had lived a strict Henrican Catholic. He was a man singularly tenacious of his own judgements. It appears doubtful as to how much he realized the growth of Protestant ideas among the leaders of the Court about him. He had been a generous master to his archbishop, who accepted his guidance in the way that dogmatic facts should be presented. He must have been aware of the Protestant leanings of his wife Queen Catherine: but neither in her case nor in that of the Princess of Aragon long ago, did he show any interest in the intellectual processes of the female sex. When he was very ill both his wife and daughter were excluded from his death bed.

He had had a long reign and was leaving England with a strengthened monarchy. As a sovereign he had been responsive to his predecessors' maxims. That open hearty good will, which gave so great a popularity with his people, was intertwined with a clear and deep suspicion which was intermittent in its expression but universal in its scope. There had always been that threat, a somewhat illusory threat, to his position from the families of the White Rose. They had come down from the fifteenth century and resembled the ships before the era of ocean voyages, hard to manage and unwieldy. The organization of their households was archaic. They stood in contrast to all the slipstream of the modern State. It was inevitable that they should founder. It was a wholly unequal contest; it was inevitable that any self-respecting rat would leave a sinking vessel. Within the ambit of the Court there were no men who would have the folly to support a failing cause. Sir Thomas More was a special case and he had no contacts with the White Rose families.

And then the King had his own creation, the Tudor aristocracy. He was, if one includes the shower of titles provided for by his will, the creator of almost all the Tudor earldoms. It was a buoyant England and money flowed about the Tudor Court.

As far as his duties as a King of England were concerned, it is probable that he was satisfied. He had left the leaders of the nation as the guardians of the realm. Among his three children it was his son who in some respects resembled him most in temperament. He had conveyed to him his own sense of the inviolable separation of the Tudor kingship from all the courtiers who would support it. This would be seen by the way in which the child King recorded in his diary the execution of his uncle the Protector Somerset: even as a boy he showed that no one was close enough to gain his trust. The king could well envisage the years of his son's reign stretching out before him, the marriage in due time with the Queen of Scotland.

The first part of the century was drawing to a close. At Rambouillet the King of France lay dying, he would not last until the coming of the spring. The Reformed Churches had entered a new phase; Luther was dead. The old Farnese Pope was failing too, but that mattered very little; he belonged to that succession of the sixteenth-century Popes, who did not understand the realm of England. The world had been different in the days of the King's youth, when the Medicean pontiffs had been reigning.

In his family King Henry was in some ways isolated. His younger sister the Queen of France had died long ago and his elder sister, whom he had never cared for, had died in Scotland at Methven Castle in 1541. His courtiers were also ageing. Sir Anthony Denny, who was perhaps closest to him in his last years, was already forty-six. The young could mean little to him in his life of pain. There is no evidence as to his degree of concern with the process against the Duke of Norfolk; there are some notes in the King's writings on the charges against the Earl of Surrey. If these charges may seem to us now as inconsistent, we should remember the clouding of the

King's mind by his suffering in these last months. But one thing never failed him, obedience and respect.

It can hardly be denied that there now lay about the King and still more around his reign the element of terrestrial greatness. The Navy was beginning and there had emerged a race of skilful and enterprising English seamen. Cromwell had left to him the core of a civil service of English laymen. It is not surprising that the King should have received the tribute of an unfeigned loyalty.

Gratitude was not in his nature: it had never been conspicuously present in any member of his royal house. It flowered in an arid fashion in his elder daughter. Gratitude was not able to co-exist with his high concept of the claims of monarchy upon his subjects.

It appears that the King had little contact with his later bishops, except for Cranmer, who was in a special sense created by him. Gardiner he disliked and many of the recent prelates were distasteful to a prince who had been brought up in the urbane and worldly care of the old Cardinal. He had never specially liked the various types of friar which had appealed to his first wife; these had now vanished.

The King was above all very English. His knowledge and that of his advisers of the lands beyond the Channel was for the most part sketchy. The Cardinal alone had had a schematic sense of all the foreign States; but in any case that had been the over-spill of fifteenth-century Europe. It had no modern relevance. The King's first marriage with the Princess of Aragon brought in a maze of foreign relatives. It was years since he had given any thought to them, save for the Emperor.

By race he was English in the sense that only his Yorkist predecessors had been before him. His ancestral lines ran back to English forbears or to the Anglo-French of the old monarchy. To this there were two exceptions, his paternal great-grandfather and his wife. Owen Tudor came from the Tudors of Penmynydd, an old Welsh stock, and he had married Catherine of Valois, a princess of the royal house of France. It is curious that, although they came from a Welsh family, none of the sovereigns of the House of Tudor ever visited the principality except Henry VII, when he landed at Milford Haven to claim the throne.

The King loved riding through that soft country of the South of

England. He was attached to Windsor Castle as also to his palaces by the riverside, to Hampton Court and Westminster and to Greenwich, which he called Placentia, where the stream broadened to the sea.

Henry VIII had been a great King of the out-of-doors. This is what made the happiness of his carefree youth in the years before the execution of the Duke of Buckingham. The last period of his life was very painful through his ulcered leg. There was now little happiness, but there remained the fact of his regality. One senses that his religious position made him lonely. He believed so clearly in that Catholic, but anti-Papalist, thought he had long followed. From one side this may be seen as transitional; but he did not move outside his own transition. The upper-class England in which he was embedded was, considered in general terms, not half so religious as its own sovereign. These last pages suggest how I conceive him. The terms in which he disposed of his remains in his will may here be quoted. 'He bequeths his soul to God, who in the person of His Son redeemed it and for our better remembrance thereof left here with us in this Church Militant the consecration and administration of His precious Body and Blood and he desires the Blessed Virgin and the holy company of Heaven to pray for him and with him while he lives and in the time of his passing hence. He desires that he be laid in the choir of his college at Windsor and that an altar shall be founded for the saying of daily Mass, while the world shall endure.'

Appendices

Appendices

Select Chart Pedigrees

o

I   The Old Royal House

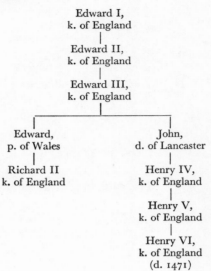

Edward I,
k. of England

Edward II,
k. of England

Edward III,
k. of England

Edward,
p. of Wales

Richard II
k. of England

John,
d. of Lancaster

Henry IV,
k. of England

Henry V,
k. of England

Henry VI,
k. of England
(d. 1471)

II   The Beaufort Descents

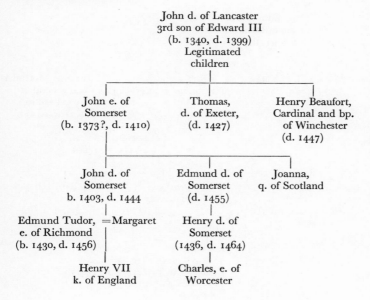

John d. of Lancaster
3rd son of Edward III
(b. 1340, d. 1399)
Legitimated
children

John e. of   Thomas,   Henry Beaufort,
Somerset   d. of Exeter,   Cardinal and bp.
(b. 1373?, d. 1410)   (d. 1427)   of Winchester
                                                (d. 1447)

John d. of   Edmund d. of   Joanna,
Somerset   Somerset   q. of Scotland
b. 1403, d. 1444   (d. 1455)

Edmund Tudor, =Margaret   Henry d. of
e. of Richmond   Somerset
(b. 1430, d. 1456)   (1436, d. 1464)

         Henry VII   Charles, e. of
      k. of England   Worcester

III   The 'White Rose' Families

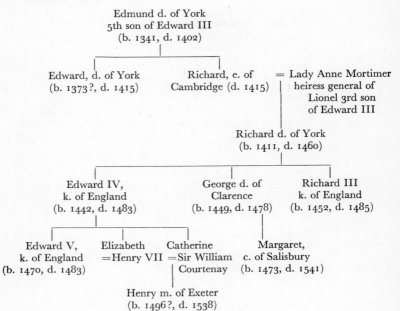

Edmund d. of York
5th son of Edward III
(b. 1341, d. 1402)

Edward, d. of York
(b. 1373?, d. 1415)

Richard, e. of   = Lady Anne Mortimer
Cambridge (d. 1415)   heiress general of
Lionel 3rd son
of Edward III

Richard d. of York
(b. 1411, d. 1460)

Edward IV,
k. of England
(b. 1442, d. 1483)

George d. of
Clarence
(b. 1449, d. 1478)

Richard III
k. of England
(b. 1452, d. 1485)

Edward V,
k. of England
(b. 1470, d. 1483)

Elizabeth
=Henry VII

Catherine
=Sir William
Courtenay

Margaret,
c. of Salisbury
(b. 1473, d. 1541)

Henry m. of Exeter
(b. 1496?, d. 1538)

IV The Dukes of Buckingham

```
                    Thomas, d. of Gloucester,
                    e. of Essex and Buckingham
                    (youngest son of Edward III)
                                  |
    Edmund Stafford,=   Anne   =  William Bourchier,
    e. of Stafford       |        C. of Eu          |
                         |                          |
                         |            ┌─────────────┴──────────────┐
                    Humphrey,      Henry Bourchier,            Thomas,
                    d. of Buckingham   e. of Essex         Cardinal Bourchier
                    (b. 1402, d. 1460)  (b. 1404, d. 1483)  (b. 1405?, d. 1486)
                         |                   |
                    Humphrey,           Sir William
                    e. of Stafford        d.v.p.
                      (d. 1455)             |
                         |                  |
                    Henry,              Henry,
                    d. of Buckingham    e. of Essex
                    (b. 1455, d. 1483)  (b. 1471?, d. 1540)
                         |
                    Edward,
                    d. of Buckingham
                    (b. 1478, d. 1521)
```

V   The Dukes of Norfolk

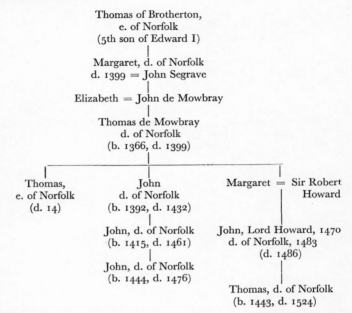

Thomas of Brotherton,
e. of Norfolk
(5th son of Edward I)
|
Margaret, d. of Norfolk
d. 1399 = John Segrave
|
Elizabeth = John de Mowbray
|
Thomas de Mowbray
d. of Norfolk
(b. 1366, d. 1399)

Thomas,
e. of Norfolk
(d. 14)

John
d. of Norfolk
(b. 1392, d. 1432)
|
John, d. of Norfolk
(b. 1415, d. 1461)
|
John, d. of Norfolk
(b. 1444, d. 1476)

Margaret = Sir Robert
Howard
|
John, Lord Howard, 1470
d. of Norfolk, 1483
(d. 1486)
|
Thomas, d. of Norfolk
(b. 1443, d. 1524)

Margaret Duchess of Norfolk was created a life-peeress in 1397 when her grandson was created Duke of Norfolk. On the extinction of this line Lord Howard was created Duke of Norfolk. The title was extinguished at his death. It was restored in 1514 with the precedency of 1397.

VI   Howard Connections

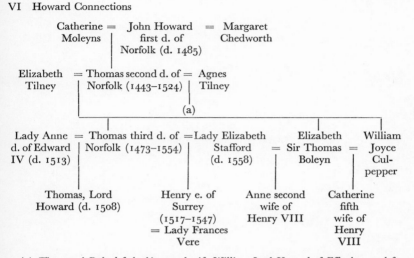

(a) *The second Duke left by his second wife William Lord Howard of Effingham and four daughters the Countesses of Oxford, Sussex, Derby and Bridgwater. The last-named was first married to Sir Rhys ap Gruffydd. The third Duke left by his second wife an only daughter the Duchess of Richmond.*

Select Bibliography

I PRIMARY SOURCES

Calender of State Papers, Venetian, ed. Rawdon Brown (1864–).

Cavendish, George, *The Life and Death of Cardinal Wolsey*, ed. R. S. Sylvester (Early English Text Society, 1959).

Chronicle of Calais (Camden Society, 1845).

Chronicle of Henry VIII of England, in Spanish by an unknown hand, trans. and ed. M. A. S. Hume (1889).

Day Book of John Dorne, ed. C. R. L. Fletcher (Oxford Historical Society), vol. V (1885).

Episcopal Court, 1514–1520, ed. Margaret Bowker (Lincoln Record Society, 1969).

Fighting Instructions, 1530–1816, ed. Julian S. Corbett (Navy Record Society), vol. XXIX (1905).

Fitzherbert, Sir Anthony (or John), *Booke of Husbandrye* (1523).

Gardiner, Stephen, *Letters*, ed. J. A. Muller (1933).

Hall, Edward, *Henry VIII*, ed. C. Whibley (1904).

Itinerary of John Leland, ed. Lucy Toulmin Smith (1907).

Letters and Papers, Foreign and Domestic, of the Reign of Henry VIII, 1509–47, ed. Brewer, Gairdner and Brodie (1862–1910, 1920).

Letters and Papers relating to the War with France, 1512–13, ed. M. Alfred Spont (Navy Records Society), vol. X (1897).

More, Thomas, *English Works*, ed. W. E. Campbell (1932).

Naval Accounts and Inventories in the reign of Henry VII, ed. M. Oppenheim (Navy Record Society), vol. VIII (1896).

Paston Letters, 1422–1509, ed. James Gairdner (1904).

Testamenta Vetusta, vol. II, ed. Nicholas Harris Nicolas (1826).

Tottel's Miscellany, ed. Hyder E. Rollins (1929).

Polydore Vergil, *Anglica Historia*, ed. D. Hay (Camden Society, 1950).

II SECONDARY SOURCES

Armstrong, C. A. J., 'The Piety of Ciceley, Duchess of York', in *For Hilaire Belloc*, ed. Douglas Woodruff (1942).

Bowker, Margaret, *The Secular Clergy in the Diocese of Lincoln*, 1495–1520 (1968).

Carpenter, Edward, *A House of Kings: The Official History of Westminster Abbey* (1966).

Chamberlain, A. B., *Hans Holbein the Younger* (1913).

Chambers, R. W., *Thomas More* (1935).

Croft-Murray, Edward, *Decorative Painting in England, 1509–1734*, vol. I (1969).

Courthope, W. J., *History of English Poetry* (1904).

Dent, J., *The Quest for Nonsuch* (1962).

Dodds, M. H. and Ruth, *The Pilgrimage of Grace and the Exeter Conspiracy* (1915).

Dugdale, G. S. D., *Whitehall through the Ages* (1950).

Elton, G. R., *The Tudor Constitution* (1960).

——, *The Tudor Revolution in Government* (1953).

Friedmann, Paul, *Anne Boleyn* (1884).

Jourdain, Margaret, *English Decoration and Furniture of the Early Renaissance* (1924).

——, *English Interior Decoration, 1500–1830* (1950).

Jordan, W. K., *Philanthropy in England, 1480–1660* (1959).

Laird Clowes, William, ed., *The Royal Navy, a History*, vol. I (1897).

Mackie, J. D., *The Earlier Tudors* (1952).

Marcus, G. J., *The Formative Years* (1961), vol. I of *A Naval History of England*.

Mattingly, Garrett, *Catherine of Aragon* (1942).

Oppé, A. P., *English Drawings at Windsor Castle* (1950).

Oppenheim, M., *History of the administration of the Royal Navy* (1896).

Parker, K., *Holbein's Drawings at Windsor Castle* (1945).

Parmiter, G. de C., *The King's Great Matter* (1967).

Pollard, A. F., *Henry VIII* (1902).

Read, Conyers, *The Tudors* (1936).

Reynolds, E. E., *St John Fisher* (1955).

——, *The Field is Won* (1968).

Ridley, Jasper, *Thomas Cranmer* (1962).

Russell, J. G., *The Field of Cloth of Gold* (1969).

Saxl, F. L., 'Holbein and the Reformation', in *Lectures* (1957); deals with Holbein's second English visit.

Scarisbrick, J. J., *Henry VIII* (1968).

Stevens, John, *Music and Poetry in the Early Tudor Court* (1961).

Stonor, R. J., *Stonor* (1951).

Strong, Roy, *Holbein and Henry VIII* (1967).

Summerson, John, *Architecture in Britain from 1530 to 1830* (1953).

Tipping, H. Avray, *English Homes, Periods I and II*, vol. II, 1066–1558 (1937).

Thomson, Patricia, *Sir Thomas Wyatt and his Background* (1964).

Waterhouse, Ellis, *Painting in Britain from 1530 to 1790* (1953).

Williams, C. H., *William Tyndale* (1969).

Williams, Neville, *Thomas Howard 4th Duke of Norfolk* (1964). For details of the Duke's childhood, cf. *Norfolk Archaeology*, vol. VII.

Zeedveld, W. Gordon, *Foundations of Tudor Policy* (1958).

INDEX

Index

P